This document is geared towards providing exact and reliable information in regards to the topic and issue covered. The publication is sold with the idea that the publisher is not required to render accounting, officially permitted, or otherwise, qualified services. If advice is necessary, legal or professional, a practiced individual in the profession should be ordered.

Legal Notice:

Disclaimer Notice:

Please note the information contained within this document is for educational and entertainment purposes only. Every attempt has been made to provide accurate, up to date and reliable complete information. No warranties of any kind are expressed or implied. Readers acknowledge that the author is not engaging in the rendering of legal, financial, medical or professional advice. The content of this book has been derived from various sources. Please consult a licensed professional before attempting any techniques outlined in this book.

By reading this document, the reader agrees that under no circumstances are is the author responsible for any loses, direct or indirect, which are incurred as a result the use of information contained within this document, including, but not limited to, - errors, omissions, or inaccuracies.

Table of Contents

Introduction—The Lectin-Free Diet

Hello! Thanks for joining us here at, "Lectin-Free Diet Cookbook." This book is specifically written for people who have just started their lectin-free journey and those who want to cook delicious food without slaving too much in the kitchen.

The Lectin-free diet is best when you have an Instant Pot. If you recently bought an Instant Pot and you want to put it to good use and make different dishes to keep you going with your diet journey, then you have come to the right place. With this book, I hope that you can find some great ideas to jumpstart your journey.

Being a health advocate myself, I also avoid lectin in my diet as it promotes inflammation in the body. I have always thought of ways on how to cook healthy and delicious dishes until I have started using the Instant Pot. The Instant Pot has allowed me to cook different delectable and healthy dishes every day, so I never get tired of following this diet regimen even if there are certain types of food that I need to avoid.

I may not be a doctor, a nutritionist, or a chef but I am an avid fan of health and cooking. I love creating recipes that are not only delicious and healthy but also following the principles of the lectin-free diet. The recipes included in this book were developed through several trials and errors.

You will find recipes for breakfast, main entrée, side dishes, soup, and snack recipes in this eBook. All of the recipes that I have developed are compiled in this book have been tried and tested so I can assure you that they are delicious. The recipes that I have developed are not only delicious but also simple so you even the most novice kitchen neophyte can follow the recipe.

Many people think that following the lectin-free diet involves a lot of complicated science, but you don't need to be a rocket scientist to be able to understand how this diet program works. While there are so many sources that you can look up online, this book aims to simplify everything for you.

You don't need to look elsewhere for information about the lectin-free diet. Let this book serve as your one-stop guide to learning about the lectin-free diet using your Instant Pot the right way!

Have fun and enjoy cooking in the kitchen!

The Lectin-Free Diet

There are so many diet regimens that promise to make people lose weight or have better health. But didn't you know that even if you are eating healthy, your body is still prone to inflammation especially if you eat the wrong food? This is where the Lectin-Free Diet comes in.

What Is Lectin?

Lectins are sugar-binding proteins that stick to cell membranes thus they become the "glyco" part of the glycoconjugates on the cell membrane. Lectins have a way for the molecules to stick together thus affecting the cell-cell interaction particularly the cells for the immune system.

You might think that lectins are abundant in meats and processed foods, but you will be more surprised that it is abundant in raw grains and legumes. They are densely found in parts of the seed that become leaves (cotyledon) when the plant germinates and turn to a sprout. This is the reason why we don't eat sprouts of red kidney beans as they contain 70,000 units of phytohaemagglutinin–a type of lectin–that can cause poisoning. Lectin is not only restricted to grains and legumes, but they are also found in some vegetables and dairy products.

But if lectin drives inflammation in the body, why does it exist in the first place? Lectins are part of the plants' defense mechanism against pests and insects. They also protect the plant such that if the seeds are eaten, it can remain intact even if it passed through the digestive system, for later dispersal especially when the seed is eaten whole raw.

Since our digestive system doesn't digest lectins, the body naturally produces antibodies to fight them. Over millions of years, our bodies have developed antibodies to fight dietary lectins thus our responses towards it may vary. While some people can tolerate lectin, others have severe immune system response.

While lectins have a bad reputation, there are some that are beneficial as they are identified to help decrease the incidence of certain diseases. Moreover, there are types of lectins that help modulate those inflammatory responses and programmed cell death.

Foods High in Lectin

Lectins are found in all life forms but there are certain foods that contain high amounts of lectin than other foods. Below are the types of foods that contain high amounts of lectin.

Red Kidney Beans

Red kidney beans contain the highest amount of lectin among all plant-based protein sources. Although they also contain high amounts of fiber and minerals, it contains the highest levels of phytohaemaggutinin–a type of lectin. Eating raw or undercooked red kidney beans can cause vomiting, nausea, and diarrhea. In fact, you only need to eat at least 5 small beans to get negative reactions.

It is important to take note that the hemagglutinating unit (hau), which is the measure of lectin content, is very high for raw kidney beans that is between 20,000 and 70,000 hau. However, once cooked, they only contain between 200 and 400 hau, which is considered a safe level.

Soybeans

Soybeans are great sources of protein and trace minerals such as molybdenum. They also contain high amounts of isoflavones that have been linked to cancer prevention. Other studies also show that it can help lower the risk of obesity and Type 2 diabetes.

While there are so many health benefits of eating soybeans, it contains high levels of lectin. Similar to red kidney beans, lectins can be removed by cooking at high temperature. Studies show that lectins in soybeans get deactivated when boiled at 100 degrees Celsius for at least 10 minutes. On the other hand, the fermentation process can also reduce the levels of lectins by as much as 95% thus making fermented soy products like soy sauce, miso, and tempeh are good to consume. Meanwhile, sprouting can reduce lectin by 59%.

Wheat

Wheat is one of the top staple foods in the world with over 35% of the world's population relying on it. There are two types of wheat products–whole and refined wheat products. The former has high fiber content thus it is beneficial on gut healthy while refined wheat products, stripped with all its nutrients, can cause the blood sugar levels to rise rapidly.

On the other hand, there are some people who find it difficult to digest gluten–a type of wheat protein–thus giving them indigestions and other discomforts. Aside from gluten, wheat (regardless of its type) contain high amounts of lectin. Refined wheat contains 300mcg of lectin per gram of wheat while whole wheat contains only 30mcg.

Cooking wheat can deactivate lectin. Lectin found in wheat can be deactivated at temperatures lower than the boiling point (65^0C).

Peanuts

Peanuts are related to lentils and beans. They contain high amounts of polyunsaturated and monounsaturated fats thus making them good sources of energy. They also contain vitamins and minerals such as Vitamin E, biotin, and thiamine.

However, they also contain high amounts of lectin. But unlike the lectin found in other food sources, those in peanuts do not reduce by heating.

A study has found that people who consume raw or roasted peanuts, lectins were found in their blood thereby indicating that they have crossed through the gut barrier. It also increases the growth of cancer cells.

Tomatoes

Tomatoes belong under the nightshade family. They contain high amounts of vitamin C and fiber thus many nutritionists recommend an intake of 30% tomatoes daily. The antioxidant lycopene found in tomatoes also have protective benefits to the heart.

However, it contains high levels of lectins. In a study on rats, lectins found in tomatoes bind to the gut wall of the laboratory rodents and caused mild-severe allergic reactions. It is also linked to rheumatoid arthritis thus putting people who carry genes for them at high risk of developing the disease.

Potatoes

Potatoes also belong to the nightshade family and are very popular among many people as French fries. They contain high amounts of potassium, vitamin C, and folate. The skin of potatoes contains high amounts of chlorogenic acid that are associated with the reduction of heart diseases and Type 2 diabetes.

Unfortunately, potatoes contain high amounts of lectin that are resistant to heat. In fact, about 40% to 50% of lectin remains even after potatoes are cooked through.

What Happens When You Ingest Lectin?

Lectins can cause damage to the gastrointestinal tract. Naturally, the lining of the gastrointestinal tract is not damaged easily as there are cells that repair the damage if present. The synergy between the digestive system and cellular repair works efficiently that the digestive system is properly protected.

But when we consume lectins, this slows down the speed of cellular repair in the intestinal tract, so the gastrointestinal tract can't regenerate itself fast enough thus compromising the entire digestive system. This is the reason why the gut can become "leaky" thus allowing different molecules to pass back and forth in the gut wall indiscriminately. This also leads to the gut not absorbing important nutrients properly such as vitamins and minerals.

When we consume too many lectins, it signals the stomach to release its contents. This is the reason why people who have severe reactions to lectins vomit. Other people also experience stomach cramps, diarrhea, and excessive flatulence.

Aside from affecting the gut wall, lectin can also affect the immune system responses of the body. The body sees it as a destructive foreign body, so it attacks aggressively. Some people experience rashes, joint pains, and general inflammation because of the immune system responses.

The Benefits of a Lectin-Free Diet

Many scientists agree that lectins are harmful and can cause different immune system responses in the body. Older pieces of literature cited that consumption of lectin can cause autoimmune diseases such as diabetes, celiac disease, and rheumatoid arthritis. It is also linked to other conditions such as heart disease, cancer, and depression. By following a lectin-free diet, you can lower the risk of severe inflammatory responses in the body. Below are the benefits of a lectin-free diet.

It Benefits People with Food Sensitivities

Eating foods that contain lectins can cause gastric distress among so many people. As leptin is not digestible, it binds to the cell membrane of the lining of the digestive tract. Once it latches on to the cell membrane, it disrupts metabolism and causes further damage to the stomach. By restricting the consumption of lectin, it will not only benefit people with food sensitivities but in general.

Avoid Consuming Toxic Foods

Although cooking can destroy most lectin in food, it is important to avoid eating raw, soaked, or undercooked beans especially kidney beans because they are very toxic due to their high levels of lectin. But even soaking beans does not remove the lectin content. By following a lectin-free diet, you don't expose your body to potentially toxic foods.

Reduce Episodes of Peptic Ulcers

Several studies on laboratory animals show that consumption of lectin can spike the growth of opportunistic harmful bacteria in the small intestines and can strip it [intestines] from its mucous defense layer thus increasing the risk for peptic ulcers.

Avoid Further Damage on The Digestive Tract

A lectin-free diet can disrupt the physiological functions of the digestive system especially if lectin is eaten over a long period of time. A lectin-free diet may not be able to push the reset button, but it can help avoid further damage to your digestive tract.

Foods to Eat on A Lectin-Free Diet

All plants and animal products contain some types of lectin, but this does not mean that you have to avoid eating everything. While there are foods that you should avoid like the plague, there are also foods that are allowed in this diet because they contain tiny amounts of lectin thereby making the safe. Below are the types of foods that you can eat while following this diet regimen.

Protein

It is important that you get a good amount of protein daily. Make sure to consume at least 30 grams of protein daily. Below are types of proteins that are allowed in the lectin-free diet.

- Fish and shellfish: Examples include wild-caught salmon, wild sardines, fish eggs (roe), oysters, and anchovies. Another low-toxicity seafood is okay.
- Beef: Make sure that it is grass-fed and not fed by corn.
- Chicken: Chicken that is pasture-raised are okay.

- Pork: Lean pork is a good source of protein. Make sure it is organic.
- Other sources of protein: Examples include cricket flour, cooked tempeh, nutritional yeasts, and liver.
- Carbohydrates
- Below are carbohydrate sources that are acceptable in the lectin-free diet:
- Starchy foods: starchy foods from tubers such as sweet potatoes, yucca, and taro contain smaller amounts of lectin. Make sure that they are thoroughly cooked.
- Fruits: Fruits contain lectins so be sure to consume limited amounts of it. Examples of fruits that are allowed in this diet include blueberries, cherries, apples, pineapples, golden berries, papaya, citrus, mango, and mulberries.
- Other sources: Other sources of carbohydrates include carob, raw honey, and trehalose.
- Fats
- You are only allowed certain types of fats under the lectin-free diet. Examples of such fats are the following:
- Caprylic acid or MTC oil: It is the best oil for the lectin-free diet. Only take 3 to 5 tablespoons of this oil daily.
- Black cumin seed oil: This oil has anti-inflammatory benefits.
- Avocadoes: Avocadoes are always known to contain healthy fats.
- Other sources: Other sources of oil include extra virgin olive oil, ghee, hemp seeds, and avocado oil.

Vegetables

There are many types of vegetables that you can eat under this diet. Vegetables contain high amounts of nutrients as well as fiber that can benefit the physiological functions of the body. Below are examples of vegetables allowed in the lectin-free diet:

- Romaine lettuce
- Cruciferous vegetables
- Cucumber

- Celery

As long as they are not members of the nightshade family, then it is safe to consume them.

Other Condiments

There are condiments that you can use that are allowed in this diet.

- Nori powder
- Sunflower lecithin
- Mustard
- Italian seasoning
- Stevia
- Xylitol
- Other Foods to Avoid

There are certain types of foods that are not allowed in the lectin-free diet as they contain high amounts of lectin that can cause inflammation. So aside from the types of foods discussed earlier, below are other types of foods that you should not include when making lectin-free recipes.

- All vegetables belonging to the nightshade family such as peppers, goji berries, and eggplants.
- All types of legumes such as chickpeas, and lentils.
- All legume-based products such as peanut butter, and peanut oil.
- All grains and products made from flour such as bread, cakes, and butter.
- All dairy products such as milk, cheese, yogurt, and butter.
- Corn and other grains such as rice, barley, and rye should be avoided when following the lectin-free diet as they cause fatty deposits in the body.

- Avoid all types of meat that are fed with corn and grains. Instead, go for meat that is pasture-raised or grass-fed especially beef.

Other Ways to Reduce Lectin in Your Diet

There are ways on how to reduce lectin in your diet. It is important to remember these tips as this will allow you to get the most out of your food – without having to worry about lectin.

- **Cook food thoroughly:** Using heat will deactivate lectin. Just to be sure, you can benefit from using a pressure cooker. This is especially true if you are cooking beans, tomatoes, quinoa, and potatoes. The high heat generated by the pressure cooker can destroy the plant lectin. But take note that lectins in barley, spelt oats, and rye are not destroyed even if you use the highest heat setting on your pressure cooker.

- **Peel and deseed fruits and vegetables:** If you don't have a choice but to use lectin-rich foods, make sure that you peel and deseed them. Remember that the most harmful part of the plant that contains high amounts of lectin is the hull, peel, and rind. Remove them as much as possible.

- **Opt for white over brown:** If you must eat grains, choose white instead of brown. So for example, eat white rice over brown because the hull has already been removed thus decreasing the amount of lectin on food.

- **Sprout seeds, grains, and beans:** Sprouting beans, grains, and seeds reduce the lectin content of food. The longer the sprouting period, the more lectins are deactivated. So if you want to eat beans, allow them to sprout first.

- **Soak before cooking:** Soaking beans and grains is a great way to reduce the amount of lectin in food. Soak beans and grains overnight and rinse before cooking can reduce the lectins as much as 50%. Use baking soda to soaking water for better results.

- **Ferment:** Fermentation allows beneficial bacteria to convert a lot of harmful substances in food. This is the reason why even if you cannot eat raw soybeans, you are allowed to eat miso, tamari, tempeh, and natto in the lectin-free diet.

The Instant Pot

The Instant Pot is a revolutionary kitchen appliance that allows you to cook food with less time needed compared to a conventional cooking method. What makes this kitchen device special is that not only can you save time and energy, but you can also cook delicious food even if you are a kitchen neophyte. Because food is cooked at a temperature higher than 1000C, it also sanitizes your food thus reducing the number of pathogens in food.

How Does an Instant Pot Work?

The Instant Pot is one of the most advanced electronic pressure cookers in the entire globe. It allows you to cook food at different pre-cook settings thus you are not limited to cooking stews but even roasts and cakes.

Operating the Instant Pot does not involve complex technical knowledge. In fact, what you only need to remember are the pre-set buttons that are found on the control panel. Let's learn more about the buttons on the Instant Pot.

- **Adjust:** This allows you change the temperature setting inside the inner pot from low to high. Use this button with the other pre-set buttons to customize your cooking.

- **"+" or "-":** This allows you to adjust the cooking time of your food. Remember that "+" extends the cooking time while the "-" shortens the cooking time.

- **Slow Cook:** Turn your Instant Pot into a crockpot. Press the "+" or "-" buttons to extend the cooking time to a few hours.

- **Yogurt:** Use this button to make yogurt in your Instant Pot.

- **Sauté:** Turn the Instant Pot into a browning pan and sauté onions and garlic. Press the "Adjust" button to change the temperature to high for stir-frying or low for simmering sauces. The lid should not be in place when using this setting.

- **Pressure:** This button allows you to switch between low and high pressures to achieve precise cooking conditions.

- **Timer:** Cook your food at a later time.

- **Manual:** This button allows you to set the cooking time for your food. Use it with the "Adjust" and "+" or "-" buttons.

- **Keep Warm/Cancel:** Press this button to cancel or turn off the Instant Pot.

- **Meat/Stew:** Cook all types of meat dishes on high pressure for 35 minutes with this pre-set button.

- **Poultry:** Cook all kinds of poultry meat for 15 minutes as the pre-set cooking time.

- **Multigrain:** Cook all types of grains on high pressure for 40 minutes with the Instant Pot.

- **Porridge/Congee:** Cook soft rice porridge with this button for 20 minutes.

- **Steam:** Use the steam rack that comes with the Instant Pot to turn the Instant Pot into a steamer. Make sure that you use at least 1 ½ cups of water to be able to generate enough steam for cooking.

- **Rice:** The button lets you cook different types of rice.

- **Bean/Chili:** Cook bean dishes with this button.

- **Soup:** This button allows you to cook different kinds of soups within 20 minutes.

Tips and Tricks to Using the Instant Pot

As one of the most intuitive kitchen appliance, using the Instant Pot can be very easy. Below are tips on how you can maximize the use of your Instant Pot so that you can prepare delicious and lectin-free recipes.

- **Use the right setting**: Using the right pre-set button allows you to cook food perfectly while removing the guesswork.

- **Use enough liquid**: The Instant Pot requires a ½ cup of water in order to maintain enough pressure inside the cooking chamber. The liquid does not necessarily need to come from water as it can be sourced from condiments and seasonings such as vinegar and soy sauce.

- **Never fill it with too many ingredients or liquid**: Too much liquid will result in a longer time for the pressure cooker to build pressure and heat to cook food. Be sure to fill the pot with ingredients and liquid only up to the "max" line.

- **Never force open the lid**: The lid does not open if the pressure is too high so do not even think about forcing to open the lid. You can open the lid by pressing the "steam release valve" or waiting for 10 minutes to normalize the pressure inside the cooking chamber.

Lectin-Free Breakfast Recipes

Breakfast Pancakes from Cassava Flour

Serves: 4

Cooking Time: 20 minutes

Ingredients:

¼ cup water

3 tbsps melted dairy-free butter

2 large eggs

½ tsp vanilla extract

1 ¼ cups goat's milk kefir

1/8 tsp nutmeg

¼ tsp sea salt

1 tsp cinnamon

1 tbsp baking powder

2 tbsps sugar

1 cup cassava flour

Instructions:

1. In a large mixing bowl, whisk well melted dairy-free butter and eggs.
2. Stir in vanilla extract, nutmeg, salt, cinnamon, baking powder, and sugar. Whisk well
3. Add water and kefir. Whisk thoroughly.
4. Whisk in cassava flour until thoroughly blended.
5. Place pot insert, and coat bottom lightly with cooking spray, and press sauté button.
6. Once pot is hot, pour ¼ cup of the batter in pot and cook for two minutes before flipping. Cook the other side for a minute and transfer to a plate.
7. If needed, lightly grease pot with cooking spray again before adding another batch of batter. Repeat process until all batter is cooked.
8. Serve and enjoy.

Nutrition information:

Calories per serving: 224; Carbohydrates: 32.2g; Protein: 5.0g; Fat: 8.9g; Sugar: 10.9g; Sodium: 310mg; Fiber: 1.4g

Lectin-Free Breakfast Burritos

Serves: 4
Cooking Time: 10 minutes

Ingredients:

8 6-inches cassava flour tortillas

4-oz goat cheese, crumbled

6 eggs, beaten

Pepper and salt to taste

2 garlic cloves, minced

2-oz spinach, chopped roughly

2 tbsps extra-virgin olive oil

Instructions:

1. Place pot insert and press sauté button.
2. Once pot is hot, add oil.
3. Meanwhile, in a bowl, whisk well eggs. Season with pepper and salt.
4. When oil is hot, add garlic cloves and sauté for a minute.
5. Add chopped spinach and stir around until wilted, around a minute or two. Evenly spread in bottom of pot.
6. Pour in egg mixture and let it sit for two minutes before stirring it up with a spatula. Cook to desired doneness. Turn pot off and sprinkle cheese on top. Let it sit while you heat up the tortillas in the microwave.
7. To serve, evenly divide the egg mixture into the middle of the 8 tortillas, fold, and enjoy.

Nutrition information:

Calories per serving: 573; Carbohydrates: 47.4g; Protein: 24.4g; Fat: 31.7g; Sugar: 4.2g; Sodium: 301mg; Fiber: 2.6g

Easy Scrambled Eggs

Serves: 6
Cooking Time: 10 minutes

Ingredients:

1/8 tsp ground black pepper

¼ tsp salt

3 cups shredded goat cheese

5 eggs

1 10-oz package frozen chopped spinach, thawed and drained

1 onion, chopped

1 tbsp olive oil

Instructions:

1. Place pot insert and press sauté button.
2. Once pot is hot, add oil and let it heat.
3. Meanwhile, in a large bowl, whisk eggs. Season with pepper and salt.
4. Add chopped onion in pot and sauté for a minute. Stir in spinach and cooked for 4 minutes or until liquid is nearly evaporated.
5. Pour in egg and cook for 2 minutes. Scramble and cook to desired doneness or around 2 minutes more.
6. Once done cooking, turn pot off, transfer to serving plates and sprinkle cheese on top.
7. Serve and enjoy.

Nutrition information:

Calories per serving: 360; Carbohydrates: 5.0g; Protein: 23.2g; Fat: 27.7g; Sugar: 1.9g; Sodium: 557mg; Fiber: 1.7g

Lectin-Free Instant Pot Omelet

Serves: 4
Cooking Time: 15 minutes

Ingredients:

Pepper and salt to taste
½ cup shredded goat cheese
¼ cup A2 milk
8 eggs
1 cup chopped cooked ham
½ onion, chopped
2 tbsps dairy-free butter
2 cups broccoli florets

Instructions:

1. Place pot insert and press sauté button.
2. Meanwhile, in a large mixing bowl whisk well eggs, salt and pepper. Stir in milk and mix thoroughly.
3. Once pot is hot, add dairy-free butter and let it melt.
4. Add onion and sauté for 2 minutes. Add broccoli florets and ham. Sauté for 4 minutes.
5. Pour in eggs and let it sit for 4 minutes. Begin to scramble the eggs and cook for another 3 minutes or to desired doneness.
6. When eggs are done, turn pot off and sprinkle cheese on top. Cover and let it sit for 3 minutes or until cheese begins to melt.
7. Divide evenly, serve and enjoy.

Nutrition information:

Calories per serving: 451; Carbohydrates: 10.2g; Protein: 34.1g; Fat: 30.2g; Sugar: 2.8g; Sodium: 848mg; Fiber: 0.2g

Potato Cauliflower Curry (Aloo Gobi)

Serves: 2

Cooking Time: 30 minutes

Ingredients:

1 large sweet potato, peeled and diced

½ tsp salt

2 tsps chili powder

2 tsps ground cumin

1 tbsp garam masala

1 tbsp grated ginger

1 onion, chopped finely

1 medium head cauliflower, chopped into florets

2 tbsps olive oil

½ cup water

Instructions:

1. Place pot insert and press sauté button.
2. Once pot is hot, add oil and heat for a minute.
3. Stir in ginger and onions. Sauté for 3 minutes.
4. Add chili powder, cumin, and garam masala. Stir fry for a minute.
5. Stir in sweet potato. Season with salt. Cook for 8 minutes while stirring occasionally.
6. Add ½ cup water and deglaze pot. Stir in cauliflower.
7. With a glass lid that would fit on your pot, cover pot and cook for ten minutes. Stir occasionally.
8. Food is done cooking when sweet potato is tender.
9. Press cancel, serve and enjoy.

Nutrition information:

Calories per serving: 304; Carbohydrates: 40.5g; Protein: 6.5g; Fat: 15.0g; Sugar: 17.0g; Sodium: 750mg; Fiber: 8.3g

Lectin-Free Sweet Potato Hash

Serves: 3
Cooking Time: 20 minutes

Ingredients:

1 stalk scallions, green part only, sliced diagonally

2 cloves garlic, smashed, peeled, and minced

½ tsp black pepper

1 onion, chopped finely

½ tsp salt

½ tsp turmeric

1 tsp smoked paprika

2 tbsps olive oil

2 medium sweet potatoes, peeled and chopped finely

2 tbsps water, optional

Instructions:

1. Place pot insert and press sauté button.
2. Once pot is hot, add oil and heat for a minute.
3. Stir in sweet potatoes, onions, and garlic. Sauté for 5 minutes.
4. Stir in pepper, salt, turmeric, and paprika. Continue to sauté for another 5 minutes.
5. If needed, add 2 tbsps of water to deglaze pot and continue cooking for another 5 minutes or until sweet potatoes are tender.
6. Once sweet potatoes are tender, turn off pot, and toss in sliced green onions.
7. Let it sit for 2 minutes, serve and enjoy.

Nutrition information:

Calories per serving: 210; Carbohydrates: 30.0g; Protein: 3.7g; Fat: 9.5g; Sugar: 11.4g; Sodium: 435mg; Fiber: 4.1g

Veggie-Laden, Lectin Free Egg Scramble

Serves: 6

Cooking Time: 15 minutes

Ingredients:

1 tsp dried oregano

½ tsp garlic powder

2 stalks celery, chopped roughly

6 medium stalks asparagus, chopped into ½-inch lengths

1 stalk green onions, chopped

6 large eggs

½ cup A2 milk

1 cup cauliflower, crumbled

2 tbsps olive oil

Pepper and salt to taste

Instructions:

1. Place pot insert and press sauté button.
2. Meanwhile in a large bowl, whisk eggs and milk. Season with oregano, garlic powder, pepper, and salt. Whisk well and set aside.
3. Once pot is hot, add oil and heat for a minute.
4. Stir in celery and asparagus. Sauté for 3 minutes.
5. Add cauliflower and continue sautéing for 4 minutes.
6. Pour in eggs. Let it sit for 4 minutes and then begin scrambling eggs until cooked to desired doneness, around 3 minutes.
7. Once eggs are cooked, turn pot off, and sprinkle green onions. Let it sit covered for 2 minutes.
8. Serve and enjoy.

Nutrition information:

Calories per serving: 134; Carbohydrates: 3.4g; Protein: 7.7g; Fat: 10.0g; Sugar: 2.0g; Sodium: 284mg; Fiber: 0.9g

Serves: 4

Cooking Time: 15 minutes

Ingredients:

1 ½ cups sausage

1 cup peeled and grated sweet potato

8 eggs

1 cup chopped kale

2 tsps garlic powder

1 onion, chopped roughly

1 cup mushrooms, chopped roughly

1 1/3 cups sliced leek

1 tbsp olive oil

Pepper and salt to taste

Instructions:

1. Prepare a casserole dish that fits inside your Instant Pot and lightly grease with cooking spray, sides and bottom.
2. Place pot insert and press sauté button.
3. Once pot is hot, add oil and let it heat for a minute.
4. Add sausage, onion, and mushrooms. Sauté for 5 minutes.
5. Stir in kale and cook for 2 to 3 minutes or until wilted. Once kale is wilted, turn pot off. Transfer mixture into prepared dish. Just leave the liquid, if any, in pot and just the solid mixture is transferred in bottom of dish.
6. In a mixing bowl, whisk eggs until fluffy. Whisk in garlic powder, pepper, and salt. Pour mixture in prepared dish. Sprinkle top with chopped leeks.
7. Cover top of dish securely with foil.
8. Add 1 cup of water in pot and trivet. Place dish on top of trivet.

9. Press cancel, press steam button, cover Instant Pot, and seal. Set cooking time to 2 minutes.
10. Once done cooking allow for natural release for 5 minutes, do a quick release, and uncover pot.
11. Serve and enjoy.

Nutrition information:

Calories per serving: 375; Carbohydrates: 15.3g; Protein: 19.5g; Fat: 26.3g; Sugar: 6.2g; Sodium: 885mg; Fiber: 2.3g

Sweet Potatoes and Buffalo Chicken

Serves: 3

Cooking Time: 25 minutes

Ingredients:

Pepper and salt to taste

½ tsp garlic powder

½ tsp onion powder

16-oz sweet potatoes, diced

3 tbsps buffalo bbq sauce

3 tbsps dairy-free butter

1 onion, diced

1-lb pasture raised chicken breast, cut into 1-inch cubes

2 tbsps water

Instructions:

1. Place pot insert and press sauté button.
2. Once pot is hot, add butter and let it melt.
3. Stir in onion and sauté for 3 minutes. Add Pepper, salt, garlic powder, and onion powder. Sauté for another minute.
4. Add Chicken and potatoes. Sauté for 5 minutes.
5. Add buffalo sauce and water. Mix well.
6. Press cancel, press manual button, choose high settings, cover Instant Pot, and seal. Set cooking time to 5 minutes.
7. Once done cooking allow for natural release for 10 minutes, do a quick release, and uncover pot.
8. Serve and enjoy.

Nutrition information:

Calories per serving: 499; Carbohydrates: 38.9g; Protein: 36.0g; Fat: 22.0g; Sugar: 9.2g; Sodium: 287mg; Fiber: 4.4g

Lettuce Wraps Asian Style

Serves: 8
Cooking Time: 20 minutes

Ingredients:

2 tsps sesame oil

1 bunch green onions, chopped

1 8-oz can water chestnuts, drained and chopped finely

2 tsps minced pickled ginger

1 tbsp rice wine vinegar

1 tbsp soy sauce

2 cloves fresh garlic, minced

¼ cup hoisin sauce

1 large onion, chopped

1 tbsp olive oil

1-lb grass fed ground beef

16 Butter lettuce leaves

Instructions:

1. Place pot insert and press sauté button.
2. Meanwhile, in a small bowl whisk well sesame oil, green onions, rice wine vinegar, soy sauce, and hoisin sauce. Set aside.
3. Once pot is hot, add olive oil and heat for a minute.
4. Once oil is hot, sauté garlic for a minute. Add ginger and sauté for another minute. Stir in ground beef, crumble and cook for ten minutes until brown and no longer pink.
5. Add water chestnuts and continue sautéing for 2 minutes.
6. Stir in green onion mixture and sauté for 5 minutes.
7. Transfer to a serving plate. Serve lettuce on the side.
8. To enjoy, scoop a good amount of ground beef mixture into middle of one lettuce leaf, roll leaf, and enjoy.

Nutrition information:

Calories per serving: 257.5; Carbohydrates: 20.4g; Protein: 11.8g; Fat: 14.5g; Sugar: 4.3g; Sodium: 201mg; Fiber: 3.4g

Smokies Wrapped in Bacon

Serves: 8
Cooking Time: 4 hours

Ingredients:
¾ cup brown sugar
1 14-oz package beef cocktail wieners, organic
1-lb sliced bacon cut into thirds

Instructions:
1. Wrap each wiener in sliced bacon.
2. Place pot insert and add all ingredients.
3. Press slow cook button, cover Instant Pot, and seal. Set cooking time to 4 hours on low.
4. Once done cooking serve and enjoy.

Nutrition information:
Calories per serving: 506; Carbohydrates: 21.9g; Protein: 26.2g; Fat: 34.3g; Sugar: 20.8g; Sodium: 1497mg; Fiber: 0g

High Protein Breakfast Casserole

Serves: 6
Cooking Time: 25 minutes

Ingredients:

8 eggs

Pepper and salt to taste

1-lb sausage, organic

½ cup A2 milk

1 stalk green onions, sliced thinly

1 onion, chopped

1 tsp garlic powder

1 tbsp olive oil

Instructions:

1. Place pot insert and press sauté button.
2. Once pot is hot, add oil and heat for a minute.
3. Add sausage, crumble and sauté for 8 minutes until no longer pink.
4. Stir in onions and garlic powder. Sauté for 5 minutes. Turn off pot.
5. In a large bowl, whisk eggs until fluffy. Pour in milk and season with pepper and salt.
6. In a heatproof dish that fits inside the Instant Pot, lightly grease with cooking spray.
7. Transfer cooked sausage in bottom of dish, leaving the oils in the pot. Pour eggs over sausage. Sprinkle green onions. Securely cover top of dish with foil.
8. Add a cup of water in pot, place a trivet, and put the dish on the trivet.
9. Press the steam button, cover Instant Pot, and seal. Set cooking time to 3 minutes.

10. Once done cooking allow for natural release for 5 minutes, do a quick release, and uncover pot.
11. Serve and enjoy.

Nutrition information:

Calories per serving: 320; Carbohydrates: 11.0g; Protein: 22.3g; Fat: 22.2g; Sugar: 2.1g; Sodium: 959mg; Fiber: 2.5g

Broccoli and Ham Casserole

Serves: 4

Cooking Time: 20 minutes

Ingredients:

6 eggs

2 cups small broccoli florets

¼ cup green onions, chopped

1 cup asparagus spears sliced into ¼-inch lengths

1 onion, chopped

1 cup mushrooms, chopped

1 cup ham, chopped

1 tsp garlic powder

2 tbsps olive oil

Instructions:

1. Place pot insert and press sauté button.
2. Once pot is hot, add oil and heat for a minute.
3. Sauté onion and mushrooms for 5 minutes.
4. Stir in broccoli florets, asparagus spears, and ham for 3 minutes. Turn pot off.
5. In a mixing bowl, whisk eggs.
6. Lightly grease a heatproof dish that fits inside Instant Pot.
7. Transfer mushroom mixture into the dish leaving the liquid in the pot if any and spread mixture evenly in dish.
8. Pour eggs over. Securely cover with foil.
9. Add a cup of water in pot, place trivet, and put dish on top of trivet.
10. Press cancel steam button, cover Instant Pot, and seal. Set cooking time to 3 minutes.

11. Once done cooking allow for natural release for 5 minutes, do a quick release, and uncover pot.
12. To serve, sprinkle green onions on top and enjoy.

Nutrition information:

Calories per serving: 260; Carbohydrates: 7.0g; Protein: 15.5g; Fat: 19.2g; Sugar: 2.8g; Sodium: 458mg; Fiber: 2.1g

Breakfast Pesto Egg Roll

Serves: 4

Cooking Time: 10 minutes

Ingredients:

4 8-inches cassava flour tortillas

6 eggs

10-oz package frozen spinach, thawed and drained

1 tsp garlic powder

1 tsp onion powder

Salt and pepper to taste

1 tbsp olive oil

2 tbsps pesto sauce

Instructions:

1. Place pot insert and press sauté button.
2. Meanwhile, in a bowl whisk eggs until fluffy. Whisk in garlic powder, onion powder, salt, and pepper. Set aside.
3. Once pot is hot, add oil and heat for a minute.
4. Stir in spinach and sauté for 3 minutes until heated through and liquid has evaporated. Pour in egg mixture and let it sit for 3 minutes.
5. Meanwhile, heat cassava flour tortillas in microwave according to package instructions.
6. Scramble the egg mixture in pot and cook for another 2 minutes or to desired doneness.
7. To serve, evenly divide egg mixture into four, place ¼ of egg mixture on one side of tortilla, spread ½ tbsp of pesto sauce on the other side of the tortilla, roll tortilla, and enjoy.

Nutrition information:

Calories per serving: 374; Carbohydrates: 48.0g; Protein: 13.4g; Fat: 14.8g; Sugar: 2.8g; Sodium: 526mg; Fiber: 4.3g

Cauliflower Breakfast Rice

Serves: 2
Cooking Time: 15 minutes

Ingredients:
3 eggs, whisked
2 cups cauliflower, crumbled
1 stalk green onions, sliced thinly
1 tsp garlic powder
Salt and pepper to taste
1 tbsp olive oil

Instructions:
1. To crumble cauliflower, chop off stems and leaves and break into florets. Place florets in blender and pulse. Do not over-pulse or else it becomes mushy.
2. Place pot insert and press sauté button.
3. Once pot is hot, add oil and heat for a minute.
4. Pour eggs, scramble and cook for 5 minutes. Transfer to a bowl and shred with two forks.
5. Add crumbled cauliflower to pot. Season with garlic powder, salt, and pepper. Continue sautéing for 5 minutes until tender yet a little bit crunchy.
6. Mix in green onions and shredded egg. Toss for a minute.
7. Serve and enjoy.

Nutrition information:
Calories per serving: 188; Carbohydrates: 7.3g; Protein: 10.7g; Fat: 13.4g; Sugar: 2.6g; Sodium: 709mg; Fiber: 2.4g

Lectin-Free Main Meal Recipes

Bowl of Chili Lectin-Free

Serves: 8

Cooking Time: 6 hours and 20 minutes

Ingredients:

8 tbsps sour cream, divided

¼ cup scallions

½ lime, cut into wedges

2 tsps coconut aminos

2 tsps red wine vinegar

1 15-oz can sweet potato puree

3-oz pine nuts

2 cups grass-fed beef broth

A pinch of ground cloves

¼ tsp ground cinnamon

2 tsps ground cumin

2 tbsps chili powder

3 celery ribs, diced finely

1 onion, diced finely

4 garlic cloves, minced

Pepper and salt to taste

2-lbs grass fed ground beef

1 tbsp olive oil

Instructions:

1. Place pot insert and press browning button.

2. Once pot is hot, add oil and heat for a minute.
3. Add garlic and sauté for a minute. Stir in onion and sauté for 2 minutes. Add beef, crumble and sauté for 10 minutes or until cooked.
4. Season with ground cloves, cinnamon, cumin, pepper, salt, and chili powder. Cook for 2 minutes.
5. Stir in celery, coconut aminos, red wine vinegar, sweet potato puree, pine nuts, and broth. Mix well
6. Press cancel, press slow cook button, cover Instant Pot, and allow to vent steam. Set cooking time to 6 hours on medium settings.
7. Serve with a tablespoon of sour cream, lemon wedge, and a sprinkle of green onions per bowl.
8. Enjoy.

Nutrition information:

Calories per serving: 464; Carbohydrates: 22.3g; Protein: 25.0g; Fat: 31.6g; Sugar: 7.2g; Sodium: 763mg; Fiber: 3.4g

Serves: 4

Cooking Time: 30 minutes

Ingredients:

4 tbsps Organic sour cream for serving

4 tbsps olive oil

½ cup cassava flour

2-oz crumbled goat cheese

Pepper and salt to taste

½ tsp ground cumin

3 cloves garlic, chopped

1 bunch Swiss chard, stemmed and torn

Instructions:

1. In food processor, pulse ¼ tsp pepper, ½ tsp salt, cumin, garlic, and Swiss chard until chopped finely. Transfer to a bowl.
2. Add flour and goat cheese to Swiss chard mixture and blend well. Evenly divide into four and form each into a patty of at least ¼-inch thick.
3. Place pot insert and press sauté button.
4. Once pot is hot, add oil and heat for 3 minutes.
5. Once oil is really hot, add patties and if needed cook in batches. Cook for 3 minutes per side. Transfer to a plate and repeat process.
6. Serve and enjoy.

Nutrition information:

Calories per serving: 273; Carbohydrates: 16.5g; Protein: 7.7g; Fat: 20.6g; Sugar: 2.4g; Sodium: 278mg; Fiber: 2.2g

Lime-Cilantro Tahini Spaghetti Squash Pasta

Serves: 2
Cooking Time: 15 minutes

Ingredients:
1 organic spaghetti squash
½ tsp salt
1 tbsp organic lime juice
1/3 cup fresh cilantro
1 ½ cup water, divided
½ cup organic tahini

Instructions:
1. Cut squash lengthwise. Scrape off and discard seeds.
2. Place pot insert, add a cup of water, and place trivet.
3. Place squash on trivet.
4. Press steam button, cover Instant Pot, and seal. Set cooking time to 7 minutes.
5. Meanwhile, make the sauce by whisking in a large bowl salt, lime juice, ½ cup water, and tahini. Mix well and set aside.
6. Once done cooking allow for natural release for 5 minutes, do a quick release, and uncover pot.
7. With a fork, scrape meat off squash into spaghetti like strands. Place in bowl of tahini dressing, toss well to coat.
8. Serve and enjoy.

Nutrition information:
Calories per serving: 500; Carbohydrates: 44.8g; Protein: 13.2g; Fat: 34.9g; Sugar: 13.0g; Sodium: 732mg; Fiber: 12.5g

Shrimps with Ginger-Honey Sauce

Serves: 4
Cooking Time: 20 minutes

Ingredients:

Pepper and salt to taste

1-lb medium shrimp, peeled and deveined

1 tsp honey

1 tsp ground ginger

¼ yellow onion, chopped

1 tsp chopped garlic

1 tbsp red pepper flakes

2 tbsps olive oil

Instructions:

1. Place pot insert and press sauté button.
2. Once pot is hot, add oil and let it heat for 3 minutes.
3. Stir in ginger and garlic. Sauté for 3 minutes.
4. Add onion and pepper flakes, continue cooking for 5 minutes.
5. Stir in shrimp, season with pepper and salt. Sauté for 8 minutes or until opaque.
6. Once done cooking, turn pot off. Add honey and toss well to coat.
7. Serve and enjoy.

Nutrition information:

Calories per serving: 160; Carbohydrates: 4.5g; Protein: 15.8g; Fat: 8.6g; Sugar: 2.3g; Sodium: 935mg; Fiber: 0.3g

Homemade Corned Beef

Serves: 8
Cooking Time: 2 hours

Ingredients:
1 cup water
6 garlic cloves, sliced
1 onion, sliced
1 tbsp olive oil
1 4-lbs flat-cut corned beef brisket + seasoning packet

Instructions:
1. Place pot insert and press sauté button.
2. Once pot is hot, add oil and let it heat for 3 minutes.
3. Add brisket and brown for 5 minutes per side to seal in the juices. Remove beef and place on a plate.
4. Add water, cloves, onion, and seasoning packet in pot. Mix well and deglaze pot.
5. Place beef brisket in pot and cover with sauce.
6. Press cancel, press manual button, cover Instant Pot, and seal. Set cooking time to 80 minutes.
7. Once done cooking allow for a complete natural release.
8. Uncover pot, slice to desired thickness, serve and enjoy.

Nutrition information:
Calories per serving: 468; Carbohydrates: 1.2g; Protein: 33.4g; Fat: 35.5g; Sugar: 0.07g; Sodium: 2,761mg; Fiber: 0.1g

Traditional Pot Roast

Serves: 8

Cooking Time: 1 hour and 25 minutes

Ingredients:

1 tsp dried rosemary

¼ cup dairy-free butter

1 cup diced onion

1 cup diced celery

1 tsp ground black pepper

2 tsps salt

3-1/2 lbs beef chuck pot roast

1 cup water

Instructions:

1. Place pot insert and press sauté button.
2. Add butter and melt.
3. Once melted, add pot roast and brown for 5 minutes per side.
4. Once done browning, add all ingredients in pot and try to deglaze sides of pot.
5. Press cancel, press manual button, cover Instant Pot, and seal. Set cooking time to 60 minutes.
6. Once done cooking allow for a complete natural release.
7. Serve and enjoy.

Nutrition information:

Calories per serving: 380.2; Carbohydrates: 4.2g; Protein: 23.8g; Fat: 29.4g; Sugar: 2.2g; Sodium: 662.2mg; Fiber: 1.1g

Delicious Beef Tenderloin

Serves: 8

Cooking Time: 1 hour and 20 minutes

Ingredients:

½ cup dairy-free butter, melted

½ tbsp salt

1 tsp pepper or more to taste

1 3-lb beef tenderloin roast

1 tbsp vinegar

1-pc star anise

1 tbsp hoisin sauce

1 cup water

1 cup mushrooms, chopped

Instructions:

1. Place pot insert and press sauté button.
2. Once pot is hot, add melted butter.
3. Place roast in pot and brown sides for 5 minutes each.
4. Once done browning, add all ingredients in pot, deglaze sides of pot and stir to mix well.
5. Press cancel, press manual button, cover Instant Pot, and seal. Set cooking time to 60 minutes.
6. Once done cooking allow for natural release for 5 minutes, do a quick release, and uncover pot.
7. Serve and enjoy.

Nutrition information:

Calories per serving: 424; Carbohydrates: 2.0g; Protein: 47.1g; Fat: 25.5g; Sugar: 1.0g; Sodium: 657mg; Fiber: 0.3g

Barbecue Korean Style (Beef Bulgogi)

Serves: 4

Cooking Time: 25 minutes

Ingredients:

2 sliced green onions, for garnish

2 tbsps olive oil, divided

½ tsp salt

¼ cup coconut aminos

1/3 cup Asian pear, grated

1 tbsp light brown sugar to taste

1 tbsp freshly grated ginger root

¼ cup yellow onion, grated

4 garlic cloves, crushed and minced

1-1/4 lbs boneless beef short ribs sliced into 1/8-inch thickness

Instructions:

1. In a large dish mix salt, coconut aminos, grated pear, brown sugar, ginger root, grated onion, and garlic. Mix well.
2. Add sliced short ribs in dish and let it marinate for at least an hour before cooking.
3. When ready to cook, place pot insert, and press sauté button.
4. Once pot is hot, add a tablespoon of oil and heat for 3 minutes.
5. In a single layer, place marinated short ribs and fry for 4 minutes per side. Cook in batches and if needed add more oil.
6. Sprinkle with green onions, serve and enjoy.

Nutrition information:

Calories per serving: 213; Carbohydrates: 8.0g; Protein: 14.9g; Fat: 13.8g; Sugar: 5.3g; Sodium: 376mg; Fiber: 0.8g

Mongolian Beef Stir Fry

Serves: 3
Cooking Time: 20 minutes

Ingredients:

¼ tsp black pepper

1 tsp salt

2 stalks green onions, sliced into 2-inch lengths

1 bunch Swiss chard, rinsed, stems removed and torn into bite size pieces

2 tbsps garlic, chopped

2 tbsps olive oil

1-lb flank steak, sliced thinly

2 tsps crushed red pepper flakes

2 tsps coconut aminos

2 tsps sugar

1 tbsp oyster sauce

2 tbsps hoisin sauce

3 tbsps hot chili oil

Instructions:

1. Place pot insert and press sauté button.
2. Once pot is hot, add oil and heat for a minute.
3. Stir in garlic and sauté for a minute.
4. Stir in thinly sliced flank steak and sauté for 5 minutes.
5. Add pepper, salt, red pepper flakes, coconut aminos, oyster sauce, hoisin sauce, and hot chili oil. Mix well and continue cooking for another 5 minutes until sauce has thickened.
6. Stir in Swiss chard and sauté until wilted, around 5 minutes.
7. Once done cooking, turn pot off, and toss in green onions.
8. Press cancel, press button, cover Instant Pot, and seal. Set cooking time to
9. Serve and enjoy.

Nutrition information:

Calories per serving: 401; Carbohydrates: 24.0g; Protein: 37.3g; Fat: 17.7g; Sugar: 13.0g; Sodium: 1617mg; Fiber: 4.8g

Salmon with Pepper and Honey

Serves: 6
Cooking Time: 3 minutes

Ingredients:
Pepper and salt to taste
6 6-oz skinless, boneless salmon fillets
¼ tsp garlic powder
½ tsp paprika
½ tsp cayenne pepper
1 tsp ground black pepper
¼ cup packed brown sugar
¾ cup honey
1 tbsp olive oil
2 tbsps lemon juice
2 tbsps white vinegar
1/3 cup coconut aminos
¼ cup pineapple juice

Instructions:
1. In a medium bowl, whisk garlic powder, cayenne pepper, 1 tsp ground black pepper, ¼ cup packed brown sugar, ¾ cup packed honey, olive oil, lemon juice, white vinegar, coconut aminos, and pineapple juice. Whisk well and set aside.
2. Generously season salmon fillets with pepper and salt.
3. Ready 6 pieces of foil that's 2.5x the length of each salmon fillet. Place seasoned salmon in middle of foil. Drizzle 1/6th of the honey mixture on top of the fillet, fold over the foil, and securely seal the sides. Repeat process for remaining fillets.
4. Place pot insert, add a cup of water, and add trivet.

5. Place foil packets side by side as well as one on top of the other.
6. Press steam button, cover Instant Pot, and seal. Set cooking time to 3 minutes.
7. Once done cooking allow for a complete natural release.
8. Serve and enjoy.

Nutrition information:

Calories per serving: 463; Carbohydrates: 48.5g; Protein: 35.7g; Fat: 14.6g; Sugar: 46.4g; Sodium: 756mg; Fiber: 0.7g

Steamed Salmon Packets

Serves: 2

Cooking Time: 8 minutes

Ingredients:

2 6-oz salmon fillets

1 tbsp fresh parsley, chopped

1 tbsp lemon juice

1 tsp ground black pepper

1 tsp salt

1 tsp dried basil

2 tbsps olive oil, divided

2 garlic cloves, minced

Instructions:

1. In a small bowl, with a fork mix well parsley, lemon juice, dried basis, and minced garlic cloves.
2. Ready two foil sheets that's 2.5x long than each fillet.
3. Pat dry salmon fillet and place one on each foil sheet.
4. Evenly season salmon with pepper and salt. Drizzle with a tablespoon of oil each. And then evenly divide the lemon juice mixture on to each foil packet, fold foil in half and seal securely.
5. Place pot insert, add a cup of water, and place trivet.
6. Place salmon packets side by side on top of the trivet.
7. Press steam button, cover Instant Pot, and seal. Set cooking time to 3 minutes.
8. Once done cooking allow for natural release for 5 minutes, do a quick release, and uncover pot.
9. Serve and enjoy.

Nutrition information:

Calories per serving: 391; Carbohydrates: 2.7g; Protein: 35.6g; Fat: 25.8g; Sugar: 0.25g; Sodium: 1,902mg; Fiber: 0.6g

Steamed Tilapia with Mango Salsa

Serves: 2
Cooking Time: 7 minutes

Ingredients:
2 tbsps lemon juice, divided
2 tbsps lime juice
1 tbsp chopped fresh cilantro
2 tbsps minced red onion
1 large ripe mango, peeled, pitted, and diced
2 6-oz tilapia fillets
½ tsp sea salt and more to taste
1 tsp ground black pepper and more to taste
1 tsp dried basil
1 garlic clove, minced
1 tbsp minced fresh parsley

Instructions:
1. On a shallow dish, mix well 1 tbsp lemon juice, ½ tsp salt, 1 tsp pepper, basil, and parsley. Add fish and cover in marinade. Let it sit and marinate for at least 30 minutes.
2. Meanwhile, make the salsa by mixing the following ingredients in a medium bowl 1 tbsp lemon juice, lime juice, cilantro, red onion, and diced mango. Season lightly with pepper and salt. Toss well to mix. Refrigerate until ready to use.
3. Once fish is done marinating, ready two foil sheets that's 2.5x longer than the length of a fillet.
4. Place one fillet on one foil sheet and evenly divide the sauce over each fillet. Fold over the foil and seal sides securely.

5. Place pot insert, add a cup of water, and add the trivet.
6. Place the foil packets side by side on top of the trivet.
7. Press steam button, cover Instant Pot, and seal. Set cooking time to 2 minutes.
8. Once done cooking allow for natural release for 5 minutes, do a quick release, and uncover pot.
9. Open packets and top with mango salsa.
10. Serve and enjoy.

Nutrition information:

Calories per serving: 244; Carbohydrates: 20.4g; Protein: 36.4g; Fat: 3.5g; Sugar: 7.8g; Sodium: 695mg; Fiber: 2.8g

Lectin-Free Fish Tacos

Serves: 6
Cooking Time: 15 minutes

Ingredients:
¼ cup sour cream
2 tbsps mayonnaise
3 tbsps lime juice, divided
A pinch of cayenne pepper or to taste
Pepper and salt to taste
½ tsp sugar
12 6-inch cassava tortillas, warmed
6 4-oz fillets tilapia
4 tbsps olive oil, divided
1 cup fresh cilantro leaves chopped, divided
1 cup peeled and diced jicama
1 cup diced red onion

Instructions:
1. In a small bowl, whisk well sour cream, mayonnaise, 1 tbsp lime juice, cayenne pepper, and sugar. Mix well. Season with pepper and salt to taste. Set aside in the fridge.
2. In a medium bowl, toss to mix remaining lime juice, jicama, red onion, and half of the cilantro leaves. Toss well to mix. Season with pepper and salt. Refrigerate.
3. Place remaining cilantro in a small bowl to serve.
4. Season fish fillet with pepper and salt.
5. Place pot insert and press sauté button.
6. Once pot is hot, add 2 tbsps of oil and heat for 3 minutes.

7. Pan fry the tilapia fillets for 3 minutes per side. Cook in to two batches. Add more oil as needed.
8. To enjoy fish tacos, place ½ of fish fillet in middle of warm cassava tortilla, drizzle with the jicama salsa, add sour cream sauce, and sprinkle more cilantro as desired.
9. Take a big bite and enjoy.

Nutrition information:

Calories per serving: 351; Carbohydrates: 36.7g; Protein: 25.0g; Fat: 12.2g; Sugar: 3.9g; Sodium: 82mg; Fiber: 3.1g

Easy Chicken Curry

Serves: 4
Cooking Time: 20 minutes

Ingredients:

3 small chicken breasts skinless and boneless, sliced into 1-inch cubes

1 bay leaf

1 15-oz can of coconut cream

2 tbsps coconut aminos

¼ tsp salt

1 tsp ground black pepper

1 tbsp turmeric powder

1 small sweet potato, peeled and diced into 1/2-inch cubes

4 cloves garlic, smashed and minced

1 onion, chopped

1 tbsp olive oil

Instructions:

1. Place pot insert and press sauté button.
2. Once pot is hot, add oil and heat for 2 minutes.
3. Add garlic and sauté for a minute. Stir in onions and bay leaf. Cook for 3 minutes.
4. Add chicken and season with pepper, salt, and turmeric. Continue sautéing for 3 minutes.
5. Stir in sweet potato and mix well. Add coconut aminos and coconut cream.
6. Press cancel, press manual button, cover Instant Pot, and seal. Set cooking time to 5 minutes.
7. Once done cooking allow for natural release for 5 minutes, do a quick release, and uncover pot.

8. Adjust seasoning if needed before serving.

Nutrition information:

Calories per serving: 353; Carbohydrates: 16.6g; Protein: 48.5g; Fat: 9.3g; Sugar: 7.7g; Sodium: 465mg; Fiber: 4.1g

Aromatic Instant Pot Whole Chicken

Serves: 12
Cooking Time: 25 minutes

Ingredients:
A dash of cayenne pepper, optional
1 tsp dried thyme
1 tbsp paprika
1 tbsp onion powder
1 tbsp garlic powder
2 tsps pepper
1 tbsp salt
1 small onion, quartered
5 garlic cloves, smashed
1 bay leaf
1 lemon
1 whole broiler chicken, around 4-lbs

Instructions:
1. In a small bowl, mix cayenne pepper, dried thyme, paprika, onion powder, garlic powder, pepper, and salt.
2. Clean and wash chicken allow to drain well.
3. Slice lemon in half. Juice half of the lemon and spread all over chicken and within chicken cavity. Slice the remaining half into circles.
4. Using half of the seasoning blend, generously season cavity of chicken. Add garlic cloves, bay leaf, lemon slices, and onion inside chicken cavity.
5. Rub the remaining dry rub all over the chicken.
6. Place pot insert, add a cup of water, and place trivet.
7. Place prepared chicken on trivet.

8. Press poultry button, cover Instant Pot, and seal. Set cooking time to 25 minutes.

9. Once done cooking allow for a complete natural release.

10. Serve and enjoy.

Nutrition information:

Calories per serving: 347; Carbohydrates: 3.7g; Protein: 38.0g; Fat: 19.1g; Sugar: 1.0g; Sodium: 685mg; Fiber: 0.7g

Moroccan Chicken Stew (Tagine)

Serves: 8
Cooking Time: 60 minutes

Ingredients:

2 tbsps honey

2 pears, cored and sliced

2 tbsps butter

½ cup water

2 tbsps fresh ginger root, peeled and minced

2 bay leaves, crushed

3 cinnamon sticks

1 tsp salt

1 tsp ground coriander

1 tsp ground cumin

1 tsp ground turmeric

1 whole chicken, cut into pieces

2 onions, peeled and sliced

2 tbsps olive oil, divided

Instructions:

1. Place pot insert and press sauté button.
2. Once pot is hot, add 2 tbsps oil and heat for 3 minutes.
3. Brown chicken for 5 minutes per side and cook in two batches. Transfer to a plate.
4. Sauté onions for two minutes. Add butter, ginger root, bay leaves, cinnamon sticks, coriander, cumin, and turmeric. Mix well and sauté for 2 minutes.
5. Add water and deglaze pot.
6. Add honey, pears, and salt. Mix well.

7. Return chicken to pot.

8. Press cancel, press poultry button, cover Instant Pot, and seal. Set cooking time to 15 minutes.

9. Once done cooking allow for natural release for 5 minutes, do a quick release, and uncover pot.

10. Serve and enjoy.

Nutrition information:

Calories per serving: 230; Carbohydrates: 11.4g; Protein: 24.7g; Fat: 9.7g; Sugar: 6.7g; Sodium: 405mg; Fiber: 3.2g

Chicken Casserole ala Florentine

Serves: 8
Cooking Time: 35 minutes

Ingredients:
2 cups shredded buffalo mozzarella cheese
2/3 cup bacon bits
4-oz mushrooms sliced
2 13.5-oz cans spinach, drained
½ cup grated Parmesan cheese
½ cup half-and-half
1 tbsp Italian seasoning
1 ¼ cups cream of mushroom soup recipe
1 tbsp lemon juice
3 tsps minced garlic
¼ cup dairy-free butter
4 skinless, boneless chicken breast halves, cut into 2-inch cubes

Instructions:
1. Place pot insert and press sauté button.
2. Once pot is hot, add butter and melt.
3. Add chicken. Sauté for ten minutes.
4. Add garlic and continue sautéing for 5 minutes.
5. Add mushrooms and Italian seasoning. Sauté for 5 minutes more.
6. Add all remaining ingredients, except for bacon bits and mozzarella cheese and mix well.
7. Press cancel, press manual button, cover Instant Pot, and seal. Set cooking time to 3 minutes.

8. Once done cooking allow for natural release for 5 minutes, do a quick release, and uncover pot.
9. Stir well, sprinkle bacon bits and mozzarella cheese. Let it sit for 5 minutes.
10. Serve and enjoy.

Nutrition information:

Calories per serving: 386; Carbohydrates: 12.0g; Protein: 47.4g; Fat: 16.0g; Sugar: 2g; Sodium: 1,004mg; Fiber: 3.3g

Serves: 4

Cooking Time: 50 minutes

Ingredients:

8 small chicken thighs, bone and skin on

1 red onion, chopped

8 garlic cloves, smashed, peeled, and chopped

1 bay leaf

¼ cup vinegar

½ cup coconut aminos

1 tbsp whole peppercorns

Instructions:

1. Place pot insert and press sauté button.
2. Once pot is hot, add chicken thighs with skin touching the pot. Cook for 8 minutes on this side. And if needed, cook in two batches. Then cook the other side for 4 minutes. Transfer to a plate. At this point, you can opt to discard skin.
3. After browning chicken, the pot now has a decent amount of oil. Sauté garlic until lightly browned around 2 minutes. Add onion and sauté until soft, around 5 minutes.
4. Return chicken to pot. Add bay leaf, vinegar, peppercorns and the coconut aminos. Mix well and deglaze pot.
5. Press cancel, press poultry button, cover Instant Pot, and seal. Set cooking time to 10 minutes.
6. Once done cooking allow for natural release for 5 minutes, do a quick release, and uncover pot.
7. Serve and enjoy.

Nutrition information:

Calories per serving: 347; Carbohydrates: 6.1g; Protein: 32.7g; Fat: 20.3g; Sugar: 2.3g; Sodium: 133mg; Fiber: 1g

Provencal Style Chicken-Balsamic

Serves: 4
Cooking Time: 50 minutes

Ingredients:

2 slices buffalo mozzarella cheese

Pepper and salt to taste

¼ tsp herbes de Provence, crumbled

2/3 cup chicken stock

2 cups cremini mushrooms, chopped

1 large shallot, chopped

4 4-oz skinless, boneless chicken breast halves, pounded flat

3 large cloves, garlic chopped

2 tsps Dijon mustard

2 ½ tbsps + 1 ½ tsps balsamic vinegar, divided

1 tsp dairy-free butter

2 tsps olive oil

Instructions:

1. In a shallow dish, whisk Dijon mustard and 2 ½ tbsps balsamic vinegar. Add chicken and turnover to coat well in sauce. Marinate for 5 minutes.
2. Place pot insert and press sauté button.
3. Once pot is hot, add butter and oil. Heat for 3 minutes.
4. Add marinated chicken, cook for 8 minutes. Then pour marinade on top of chicken and then turnover to cook the other side for another 8 minutes. Transfer to a plate and keep warm.
5. Sauté garlic, mushrooms, and shallots for 5 minutes.

6. Add chicken stock and deglaze pot. Cook for 5 minutes or until heated through. Season with pepper and salt to taste. Add remaining balsamic. Render sauce until one-half is evaporated.
7. Return chicken to pot and add mozzarella cheese on top of each breast.
8. Cook until heated through and cheese has melted.
9. Serve and enjoy.

Nutrition information:

Calories per serving: 416; Carbohydrates: 7.2g; Protein: 64.6g; Fat: 13.3g; Sugar: 1.9g; Sodium: 216mg; Fiber: 3g

Jamaican Jerk Chicken

Serves: 4

Cooking Time: 25 minutes

Ingredients:

1 ½ lbs skinless, boneless chicken breast halves, cut into 2-inch thick strips

½ tsp ground allspice

½ tsp ground nutmeg

½ tsp ground cloves

1 tbsp chopped fresh thyme

2 tbsps brown sugar

¼ cup olive oil

½ cup distilled white vinegar

¾ cup coconut aminos

1 onion, chopped

6 green onions, chopped

Instructions:

1. In blender puree until smooth and creamy the allspice, nutmeg, cloves, thyme, brown sugar, vinegar, soy sauce, onion, and green onions.
2. Transfer pureed mixture in a shallow dish. Add chicken and let it marinate for 10 minutes. Thoroughly cover chicken ins marinade.
3. Place pot insert and press sauté button.
4. Once pot is hot, add oil and heat for 10 minutes.
5. Add chicken and marinade in pot. Stir fry for 8 minutes.
6. Transfer to a plate.
7. Serve and enjoy.

Nutrition information:

Calories per serving: 385; Carbohydrates: 15.4g; Protein: 39.2g; Fat: 18.2g; Sugar: 9g; Sodium: 2,798mg; Fiber: 1.8g

Serves: 4

Cooking Time: 35 minutes

Ingredients:

1 tbsp capers

1 cup white wine

1 cup slice fresh mushrooms

1 14-oz can artichoke hearts, drained and liquid reserved

1 tbsp dairy-free butter

1 tbsp olive oil

Pepper and salt to taste

4 skinless, boneless chicken breast halves

Instructions:

1. Place pot insert and press sauté button.
2. Once pot is hot, add butter ad oil. Heat for 5 minutes.
3. Meanwhile, slice chicken breast halves in half lengthwise. Generously season with pepper and salt.
4. Brown chicken in pot for 5 minutes per side. Transfer to a plate and keep warm.
5. Add mushrooms in pot and sauté for 5 minutes until soft.
6. Add artichoke hearts and sauté for a minute.
7. Add white wine and deglaze pot.
8. Stir in reserved liquid and cooked chicken.
9. Continue cooking and simmering for 15 minutes or until sauce is rendered.
10. Turn pot off, Serve chicken in plate and sprinkle capers on top.
11. Press cancel, press   button, cover Instant Pot, and seal. Set cooking time to

Nutrition information:

Calories per serving: 312; Carbohydrates: 9.6g; Protein: 25g; Fat: 16.2g; Sugar: 1g; Sodium: 426mg; Fiber: 3.9g

Serves: 6

Cooking Time: 4 hours and 20 minutes

Ingredients:

¾ cup water

2 cups mushrooms chopped roughly

2 ½ cups cream of mushroom soup recipe

2 tbsps olive oil

¼ cup A2 milk

1 tbsp onion powder

2-lbs lean ground beef

1 tbsp garlic powder

1 tsp salt

1 tsp pepper

1 egg

Instructions:

1. In a large bowl whisk egg. Add milk, onion powder, garlic powder, salt, and pepper. Whisk well.
2. With hands, mix in ground beef and mix well. Leave for 30 minutes and then mix again with hands. Evenly divide mixture into 6 equal parts and form into patties.
3. Place pot insert and press sauté button.
4. Once pot is hot, add oil and heat for 3 minutes.
5. Cook patties for 4 minutes per side in several batches. Transfer to a plate and keep warm.
6. Add water and deglaze pot. Add mushrooms and condensed cream of soup. Mix well. Return patties to pot and stagger one on top of the other.
7. Press cancel, press slow cook button, cover Instant Pot, and do not seal. Set cooking time to 4 hours on low settings.
8. Once done cooking serve and enjoy.

Nutrition information:

Calories per serving: 450; Carbohydrates: 7.9g; Protein: 44.3g; Fat: 26.0g; Sugar: 2.0g; Sodium: 857mg; Fiber: 1.1g

Turkey Meatballs in BBQ Sauce

Serves: 12

Cooking Time: 4 hours and 20 minutes

Ingredients:

¼ cup orange marmalade

1 cup bottled BBQ sauce

1 1/2-lbs ground turkey

¼ tsp black pepper

¼ tsp salt

1 tsp Italian seasoning blend

2 tbsps finely chopped onion

1 5.3-oz non-dairy yogurt

1 egg

2 tbsps oil

Instructions:

1. In a large bowl, whisk egg. Add pepper, salt, Italian seasoning, onion, and yogurt. Mix well with hands. Evenly divide into 12 portions and form into balls.
2. Place pot insert and press sauté button.
3. Once pot is hot, add 1 tbsp oil and heat for 3 minutes. Cook meatballs in two batches and add more oil as needed. Cook each meatball for at least 10 minutes per batch.
4. Mix well marmalade and BBQ sauce in pot. Deglaze pot. Return meatballs and cover well in sauce.
5. Press cancel, press slow cook button, cover Instant Pot. Set cooking time to 4 hours on low.
6. Once done cooking serve and enjoy.

Nutrition information:

Calories per serving: 488.6; Carbohydrates: 84.3g; Protein: 21.5g; Fat: 6.2g; Sugar: g; Sodium: 2,828mg; Fiber: 3.1g

Baby Back Ribs in Instant Pot

Serves: 4
Cooking Time: 20 minutes

Ingredients:

½ cup BBQ sauce, divided

1 cup beef broth

1 rack baby back pork ribs

1 tsp ground black pepper

1 ½ tsps cayenne pepper

2 tsps garlic powder

1 tbsp paprika

1 tbsp chili powder

1 tbsp brown sugar

2 tbsps salt

Instructions:

1. Generously season ribs with pepper and salt.
2. Place pot insert.
3. Mix well beef broth, cayenne pepper, garlic powder, paprika, chili powder, ¼ cup BBQ sauce, and brown sugar.
4. Press meat button, cover Instant Pot, and seal. Set cooking time to 20 minutes.
5. Once done cooking allow for a complete natural release.
6. Transfer ribs to a roasting rack. Brush remaining BBQ sauce all over ribs and broil for 3 minutes per side.
7. Serve and enjoy.

Nutrition information:

Calories per serving: 335; Carbohydrates: 12.8g; Protein: 19.6g; Fat: 22.8g; Sugar: g; Sodium: 3,349mg; Fiber: 1.9g

Smothered Pork Chops in Mushroom

Serves: 4

Cooking Time: 25 minutes

Ingredients:

1 ¼ cups cream of mushroom soup recipe

½ lb fresh mushrooms, sliced

1 onion, chopped

1 tsp garlic salt

Pepper and salt to taste

4 pork chops

1 tbsp olive oil

Instructions:

1. Place pot insert and press sauté button.
2. Once pot is hot, add oil and heat for 3 minutes.
3. Meanwhile, season chops with salt and pepper generously. Brown in pot for 5 minutes per side. If needed, cook in batches and set aside on a plate.
4. Add onions and sauté for 2 minutes. Add mushrooms and sauté for 3 minutes while also deglazing pot.
5. Add cream of mushroom soup and mix well. Add porkchops back into pot.
6. Press cancel, press manual button, cover Instant Pot, and seal. Set cooking time to 3 minutes.
7. Once done cooking allow for a complete natural release.
8. Serve and enjoy.

Nutrition information:

Calories per serving: 357; Carbohydrates: 14.6g; Protein: 29.3g; Fat: 20.2g; Sugar: 4.1g; Sodium: 329mg; Fiber: 2.1g

Lectin-Free Side Dish, Dips, and Dressing Recipes

Stir-Fried Asparagus

Serves: 8
Cooking Time: 2 minutes

Ingredients:
½ tsp freshly ground black pepper
½ tsp salt
¼ cup chopped fresh parsley
2 tsps grated lemon zest
1 ½ cups balsamic vinaigrette salad dressing
2-lbs fresh asparagus, trimmed and cut into 2 ½-inch pieces

Instructions:
1. Place pot insert, add 2 cups of water, press manual button, cover Instant Pot, and seal. Set cooking time to 2 minutes.
2. Do a quick release, uncover pot, dump asparagus spears in boiling water, leave for a minute, and then drain. Run under cold water to stop cooking process and let it drain for 10 minutes.
3. In a Ziploc bag, mix well pepper, salt, parsley, zest, and salad dressing. Add cooled asparagus. Let it marinate for at least an hour in the fridge.
4. Serve and enjoy.

Nutrition information:
Calories per serving: 158.5; Carbohydrates: 9g; Protein: 2.5g; Fat: 13.7g; Sugar: g; Sodium: 891.5mg; Fiber: 2.2g

Sweet Potato Hummus

Serves: 6
Cooking Time: 10 minutes

Ingredients:
½ tsp salt
½ tsp pepper
2 cloves garlic, smashed and peeled
2 tbsps olive oil
¼ cup organic lime juice
¼ cup tahini
1 cup organic sweet potato, peeled and quartered

Instructions:
1. Place pot insert, add a cup of water, and add sweet potato.
2. Press steam button, cover Instant Pot, and seal. Set cooking time to 5 minutes.
3. Once done cooking allow for natural release for 5 minutes, do a quick release, and uncover pot.
4. In a blender, add salt, pepper, garlic, olive oil, lime juice, and tahini. Puree until smooth and creamy.
5. Add softened sweet potato in blender and continue pureeing until smooth and creamy.
6. Serve and enjoy.

Nutrition information:
Calories per serving: 135; Carbohydrates: 10.7g; Protein: 2.4g; Fat: 10.0g; Sugar: 2.6g; Sodium: 217mg; Fiber: 2.1g

Lectin-Free Pasta

Serves: 4

Cooking Time: 4 minutes

Ingredients:

½ tsp black pepper

½ tsp salt

1 tbsp olive oil

2 cloves garlic, smashed and peeled

2 tbsps lemon juice

¾ cup almond milk

1 ¼ cup pine nuts

2 packs Miracle Noodles

1 can artichoke hearts, drained and chopped

Instructions:

1. Place pot insert and add 3 cups of water.
2. Press manual button, cover Instant Pot, and seal. Set cooking time to 2 minutes.
3. Once done cooking do a quick release, uncover pot, and dump noodles. Let it sit there for two minutes and then drain quickly. Run under cold water to stop cooking process. Let it drain for 10 minutes.
4. In a blender, puree pepper, salt, olive oil, garlic, lemon juice, pine nuts, and almond milk. Once smooth and creamy, transfer to a bowl.
5. Add well-drained noodles to bowl and toss well to coat in sauce.
6. Serve and enjoy.

Nutrition information:

Calories per serving: 476; Carbohydrates: 40.0g; Protein: 10.7g; Fat: 33.1g; Sugar: 6.4g; Sodium: 484mg; Fiber: 4.5g

Chipotle-Style Cauliflower Rice

Serves: 2
Cooking Time: 8 minutes

Ingredients:
¼ cup fresh cilantro chopped
½ tsp black pepper
1 tsp salt
1 tbsp olive oil
2 tbsps lime juice
2 cups cauliflower rice

Instructions:

1. Chopped cauliflower into florets and then pulsed until grainy. Do not over pulsed or else it gets mushy.
2. Place pot insert and press sauté button.
3. Once pot is hot, add oil and let it heat for 3 minutes.
4. Meanwhile in a medium bowl mix well pepper, salt, lime juice, and chopped cilantro. Set aside.
5. Once pot is hot, add cauliflower rice and sauté for 5 minutes until soft yet still crunchy. Immediately transfer into bowl of lime-cilantro mixture. Toss well to coat and mix.
6. Serve and enjoy.

Nutrition information:
Calories per serving: 100; Carbohydrates: 9.6g; Protein: 2.4g; Fat: 7.1g; Sugar: 2.8g; Sodium: 1197mg; Fiber: 2.6g

Stir Fried Brussels Sprouts

Serves: 6
Cooking Time: 15 minutes

Ingredients:
½ tsp freshly ground black pepper
1 tsp salt
3 tbsps olive oil
1 ½-lbs Brussels sprouts

Instructions:
1. Ready sprouts by trimming off the ends, removing yellowed leaves, and cutting the big ones in half.
2. Place pot insert and press sauté button.
3. Once pot is hot, add oil and heat for 3 minutes.
4. Add Brussels sprouts and sauté for 5 minutes. Season with pepper and salt. Continue sautéing for 3 more minutes or until tender but not soggy.
5. Transfer to serving plates.
6. Serve and enjoy.

Nutrition information:
Calories per serving: 104; Carbohydrates: 10g; Protein: 2.9g; Fat: 7.3g; Sugar: 5g; Sodium: 344mg; Fiber: 3g

Mushroom Stir Fry

Serves: 4
Cooking Time: 20 minutes

Ingredients:
Pepper to taste
¼ tsp salt
1 tbsp teriyaki sauce
1 tbsp red cooking wine
1 clove garlic, smashed, peeled and minced
1-lb small button mushrooms
3 tbsps butter
1 tbsp olive oil
1 onion, sliced

Instructions:
1. Place pot insert and press sauté button.
2. Once pot is hot, add oil and heat for a minute.
3. Add garlic and sauté for a minute. Add onions and sauté for 3 minutes.
4. Add butter and mushrooms. Cook for 5 minutes.
5. Stir in Pepper, salt, teriyaki sauce, and cooking wine. Mix well.
6. Continue cooking for another 10 minutes until mushroom has turned into a dark brown color and is tender.
7. Serve and enjoy.

Nutrition information:
Calories per serving: 199; Carbohydrates: 5.3g; Protein: 3.9g; Fat: 19.2g; Sugar: 3g; Sodium: 376mg; Fiber: 1.2g

Butter-Balsamic Drizzled Asparagus

Serves: 4
Cooking Time: 25 minutes

Ingredients:
1 tsp balsamic vinegar
1 tbsp coconut aminos
4 tbsps butter
Pepper and salt to taste
1 bunch fresh asparagus, trimmed

Instructions:
1. Place pot insert and press sauté button.
2. Once pot is hot, add butter and melt.
3. Once butter is melted add asparagus and sauté for 5 minutes.
4. Season with pepper and salt.
5. Transfer asparagus to a serving plate.
6. Pour the butter sauce into a small bowl. Whisk in balsamic and coconut aminos.
7. Drizzle sauce all over asparagus.
8. Serve and enjoy.

Nutrition information:
Calories per serving: 77; Carbohydrates: 4.9g; Protein: 2.8g; Fat: 5.9g; Sugar: 2g; Sodium: 269mg; Fiber: 2.4g

Steamed Lemony Asparagus

Serves: 6

Cooking Time: 2 minutes

Ingredients:

Pepper and salt to taste

1 tbsp fresh parsley, chopped

2 tbsps lemon juice

3 tbsps sesame seed, toasted

1/3 cup butter

1-lb asparagus spears, ends trimmed

1 tbsp deep fried garlic

1 cup water

Instructions:

1. Place pot insert, add water, and place trivet.
2. In a heatproof dish that fits inside Instant pot, place half of butter on bottom of dish. Arrange asparagus spear in an even layer. Season with pepper and salt. Drizzle lemon juice all over. Evenly divide remaining butter on top of asparagus and sprinkle garlic all over.
3. Securely cover dish with foil.
4. Place dish on trivet in pot.
5. Press steam button, cover Instant Pot, and set cooking time to 2 minutes.
6. Once done cooking do a quick release.
7. Serve and enjoy.

Nutrition information:

Calories per serving: 131; Carbohydrates: 4.4g; Protein: 2.6g; Fat: 12.3g; Sugar: 2g; Sodium: 184mg; Fiber: 2.1g

Stir-Fried Mushroom and Brussels Sprouts

Serves: 4

Cooking Time: 25 minutes

Ingredients:

½-lb Brussels sprouts, ends trimmed and halved

1-lb small button mushrooms

1 tsp coconut aminos

¼ tsp salt

½ tsp pepper

1 sweet onion, sliced

1 tbsp olive oil

3 garlic cloves, smashed, peeled and minced

Instructions:

1. Place pot insert and press sauté button.
2. Once pot is hot, add oil and heat for 2 minutes.
3. Sauté garlic for a minute.
4. Stir in onions and cook for 5 minutes.
5. Stir in mushrooms and season with coconut aminos, salt, and pepper. Cook for 2 minutes.
6. Add Brussels sprouts and cook for 10 minutes.
7. Once mushroom and Brussels sprouts are tender, turn pot off.
8. Serve and enjoy.

Nutrition information:

Calories per serving: 111; Carbohydrates: 16.3g; Protein: 6.3g; Fat: 4.0g; Sugar: 8.0g; Sodium: 174mg; Fiber: 4.2g

Chinese Vegetable Stir-fry

Serves: 8

Cooking Time: 16 minutes

Ingredients:

1 small head broccoli, cut into florets

1-lb button mushrooms, small

1 bunch asparagus, cut into 1 ½-inch lengths

½ cup water

1 tbsp cassava flour

3 tbsps fish sauce

½ tsp ground black pepper

1 sweet onion, sliced

4 garlic cloves, smashed, peeled, and minced

1 tbsp olive oil

Instructions:

1. Place pot insert and press sauté button.
2. Once pot is hot, add oil and heat for 3 minutes.
3. Stir fry garlic for a minute and add onion. Cook for 2 minutes.
4. Stir in mushrooms, broccoli, and asparagus.
5. Season with fish sauce and black pepper. Mix well. Cook for 3 minutes.
6. Meanwhile, mix well water and cassava flour. Pour into pot.
7. Continue mixing and cooking until vegetables are fork tender, around 8 minutes more.
8. Serve and enjoy.

Nutrition information:

Calories per serving: 214; Carbohydrates: 49.7g; Protein: 7.0g; Fat: 2.4g; Sugar: 4.3g; Sodium: 19mg; Fiber: 8.2g

Lectin-Free Soup Recipes

Creamy Curry Cauliflower Bisque

Serves: 4

Cooking Time: 20 minutes

Ingredients:

1 can coconut milk

½ tsp ground black pepper

½ tsp salt

2 tbsps olive oil

2 garlic cloves, minced

1 yellow onion, chopped

5 cups cauliflower rice

1 tsp fish sauce

1 tbsp turmeric powder

1 tbsp grated ginger root

Instructions:

1. Place pot insert and press sauté button.
2. Once pot is hot, add oil and heat for 3 minutes.
3. Sauté garlic and ginger for a minute and then add onions and turmeric powder. Cook for 5 minutes.
4. Add cauliflower, coconut milk, black pepper, salt, and fish sauce. Mix well.
5. Continue simmering soup for 10 minutes.
6. With a handheld blender, puree bisque.
7. Serve and enjoy.

Nutrition information:

Calories per serving: 145; Carbohydrates: 13.2g; Protein: 3.7g; Fat: 9.7g; Sugar: 5.3g; Sodium: 507mg; Fiber: 4.3g

Serves: 4

Cooking Time: 20 minutes

Ingredients:

1 13.5-oz can coconut milk

½ tsp ground pepper

½ tsp salt

2 tsps olive oil

3 garlic cloves, minced

1 bunch asparagus stalks

3 stalks celery, chopped

½ tsp dill

Instructions:

1. Place pot insert and press sauté button.
2. Once pot is hot, add oil and let it heat up for 2 minutes.
3. Stir in garlic and sauté for a minute.
4. Add celery and asparagus. Sauté for 5 minutes.
5. Add coconut milk, ground pepper, and salt. Continue simmering for 10 minutes.
6. When vegetables are tender, puree with a handheld blender.
7. Sprinkle dill and adjust seasoning to taste.
8. Serve and enjoy.

Nutrition information:

Calories per serving: 229; Carbohydrates: 6.8g; Protein: 3.6g; Fat: 22.8g; Sugar: 1.6g; Sodium: 315mg; Fiber: 1.7g

Coconut Soup Thai Style

Serves: 6
Cooking Time: 30 minutes

Ingredients:

¼ cup chopped cilantro

Salt to taste

2 tbsps fresh lime juice

1-lb medium shrimp, peeled and deveined

½ lb fresh shiitake mushrooms, sliced

2 13.5-oz cans coconut milk

1 tbsp light brown sugar

3 tbsps fish sauce

4 cups chicken broth

2 tsps curry paste

1 stalk lemon grass, folded and tied

2 tbsps grated fresh ginger

1 tbsp olive oil

Instructions:

1. Place pot insert and press sauté button.
2. Once pot is hot, add oil and heat for 3 minutes.
3. Stir in lemon grass and ginger. Sauté for a minute.
4. Add mushrooms. Sauté for 3 minutes.
5. Stir in cilantro, coconut milk, light brown sugar, fish sauce, chicken broth, and curry paste. Mix well and bring to a simmer.
6. Once simmering, add shrimps and continue simmering for 8 minutes or until shrimps are pink.
7. Add salt if needed.
8. Serve and enjoy.

Nutrition information:

Calories per serving: 379; Carbohydrates: 14.7g; Protein: 46.3g; Fat: 14.5g; Sugar: 5.1g; Sodium: 1555mg; Fiber: 2.1g

Crab and Shrimp Bisque

Serves: 6

Cooking Time: 20 minutes

Ingredients:

½ cup white wine

½ lb pre-cooked crab meat

½ lb medium shrimp, peeled and deveined

1 cup dairy-free yogurt

2 tbsps finely chopped onion

1 tsp chicken bouillon granules

¼ tsp white pepper

½ tsp salt

2 tbsps cassava flour

½ cup water

2 tbsps dairy-free butter

Instructions:

1. Place pot insert and press sauté button.
2. Once pot is hot, add butter and let it melt.
3. Stir in onion and shrimp. Sauté for 5 minutes.
4. Stir in crab meat, bouillon, white pepper, and salt. Mix well and cook for 3 minutes.
5. Add white wine and yogurt. Mix well and bring to a simmer while frequently stirring pot, around 10 minutes.
6. Once simmering, with a handheld blender, puree bisque until smooth.
7. In a small cup, mix well cassava flour and water. Pour into bisque and continue cooking and mixing until thick and creamy.
8. Serve and enjoy.

Nutrition information:

Calories per serving: 164; Carbohydrates: 13.0g; Protein: 14.3g; Fat: 6.1g; Sugar: 7.8g; Sodium: 584mg; Fiber: 1.1g

Beef Soup Filipino Style

Serves: 5

Cooking Time: 35 minutes

Ingredients:

2-lbs beef stew meat, cut into 2-inch cubes

1 package bone marrow, optional

1 onion, quartered

6 garlic cloves, smashed and peeled

1 tbsp whole peppercorns

1 stalk green onions, sliced into ½-inch lengths

3 Bok choy, leaves separated

1 beef bouillon cube

2 tbsps fish sauce

½ tsp salt

6 cups water, divided

Instructions:

1. Place pot insert.
2. Add all ingredients except for green onions and bok choy.
3. Press button, cover Instant Pot, and seal. Set cooking time to 20 minutes
4. Once done cooking allow for a complete natural release.
5. Open pot and if desired, skim off and discard layer of oil.
6. Add bok choy and onions. Let it sit for 2 minutes.
7. Taste broth and if needed add more fish sauce.
8. Serve and enjoy.

Nutrition information:

Calories per serving: 434; Carbohydrates: 6.0g; Protein: 43.4g; Fat: 26.8g; Sugar: 2.1g; Sodium: 427mg; Fiber: 1.4g

Cream of Mushroom Soup

Serves: 4

Cooking Time: 15 minutes

Ingredients:

¼ tsp pepper

½ tsp salt

1 cup A2 milk

1 cup chicken broth

4 tbsps cassava flour

3 tbsps dairy-free butter

2 garlic cloves, smashed and minced

¼ cup sweet onions diced finely

8-oz fresh sliced mushrooms

Instructions:

1. Place pot insert and press sauté button.
2. Once pot is hot, add butter and melt.
3. Stir in onions, garlic, and mushrooms. Sauté for 5 minutes.
4. Add pepper, salt, and chicken broth. Mix well.
5. Press cancel, press manual button, cover Instant Pot, and seal. Set cooking time to 3 minutes.
6. Once done cooking allow for natural release for 5 minutes, do a quick release, and uncover pot.
7. Meanwhile, whisk well cassava flour and milk. Once pot is opened, stir in slurry while continuously whisking soup until creamy.
8. Serve and enjoy.
9. **for substitutions, 1 can of cream of mushroom soup is equal to 1 ¼ cups of this recipe.

Nutrition information:

Calories per serving: 223; Carbohydrates: 11.4g; Protein: 17.3g;

Chicken Soup Recipe from the Philippines

Serves: 2

Cooking Time: 30 minutes

Ingredients:

1 Cornish hen, chopped into pieces

1 chicken bouillon

¼ tsp salt

½ tsp cracked pepper

4 garlic cloves, smashed and minced

1 medium onion, chopped

1-inch thumb ginger, peeled and sliced thinly

1 chayote, peeled, deseeded

2 tsps fish sauce

1 package frozen moringa leaves, optional

1 stalk lemongrass

1 tsp olive oil

3 cups water

Instructions:

1. Slice the chayote into quarters, lengthwise. And then each quarter, slice again diagonally in ½-inch thickness. Set aside.
2. The lemongrass, peel 1 leaf off the whole length and fold into 2-inch length. Tie with a roasting tie and set aside.
3. Place pot insert and press sauté button.
4. Once pot is hot, add oil and heat for 2 minutes.
5. Sauté garlic until lightly browned around 2 minutes.
6. Stir in onions, ginger, and tied lemongrass. Sauté for 4 minutes.
7. Add chicken. Season with pepper and salt. Sauté for 5 minutes.

8. Stir in chicken bouillon, chayote, fish sauce, and water. Stir well to deglaze pot.

9. Press cancel, press poultry button, cover Instant Pot, and seal. Set cooking time to 5 minutes.

10. Once done cooking allow for natural release for 10 minutes, do a quick release, and uncover pot.

11. Discard lemon grass and stir in frozen moringa leaves. Stir to mix and cook until heated through, around 2 minutes.

12. Serve and enjoy.

Nutrition information:

Calories per serving: 252; Carbohydrates: 19.4g; Protein: 28.9g; Fat: 7.0g; Sugar: 6.7g; Sodium: 892.5mg; Fiber: 3.4g

Lectin-Free Zuppa Toscana

Serves: 4

Cooking Time: 20 minutes

Ingredients:

¼ bunch fresh spinach

2 cups creamy mushroom soup recipe

1 large sweet potato, peeled and sliced thinly

1 chicken bouillon

2 cups water

1 tbsp minced garlic

1 large onion, diced

4 slices bacon

1 ¼ tsps crushed red pepper flakes

1-lb mild Italian sausage

Instructions:

1. Slice sausage lengthwise in half and then slice into ¼-inch thick half-moons. Set aside.
2. Place pot insert and press sauté button.
3. Once pot is hot, add bacon and fry until crisped, around 5 minutes per side. Remove from pot, let it cool, crumble bacon, and then set aside.
4. In pot, sauté onion and garlic in bacon fat for 5 minutes.
5. Stir in sliced sausage and sweet potato. Add chicken bouillon, water, and pepper flakes. Mix well.
6. Press cancel, press manual button, cover Instant Pot, and seal. Set cooking time to 3 minutes.
7. Once done cooking allow for natural release for 5 minutes, do a quick release, and uncover pot.
8. Stir in fresh spinach and creamy mushroom soup. Mix well and cook until heated through, around 3 minutes.
9. Serve and enjoy.

Nutrition information:

Calories per serving: 471; Carbohydrates: 19.1g; Protein: 24.2g; Fat: 33.1g; Sugar: 5.7g; Sodium: 1368mg; Fiber: 2.4g

Traditional Broccoli Cheese Chowder

Serves: 6

Cooking Time: 15 minutes

Ingredients:

1 cup water

2 tbsps cassava starch

1 tbsp garlic powder

2 cups A2 milk

2 14.5-oz cans chicken broth

1 16-oz package frozen chopped broccoli

1 onion, chopped

½ cup dairy-free butter

2 cups goat cheese, shredded

Instructions:

1. Place pot insert.
2. Add water, garlic powder, chicken broth, broccoli, onion, and butter.
3. Press manual button, cover Instant Pot, and seal. Set cooking time to 2 minutes.
4. Once done cooking allow for natural release for 5 minutes, do a quick release, and uncover pot.
5. With a handheld mixer, puree broccoli until smooth.
6. Stir in cheese. Cook and stir frequently until melted and incorporated.
7. Meanwhile, in a bowl, whisk well milk and cassava starch. Pour into pot to thicken chowder.
8. Once chowder has thickened, serve and enjoy.

Nutrition information:

Calories per serving: 306; Carbohydrates: 14.7g; Protein: 14.7g; Fat: 21.7g; Sugar: 8.1g; Sodium: 671mg; Fiber: 2.8g

Mushroom Soup Hungarian Style

Serves: 6

Cooking Time: 20 minutes

Ingredients:

½ cup sour cream

¼ cup chopped fresh parsley

2 tsps lemon juice

Pepper to taste

1 tsp salt

3 tbsps cassava flour

1 cup A2 milk

2 cups chicken broth

1 tbsp coconut aminos

1 tbsp paprika

2 tsps dried dill weed

1-lb fresh mushrooms, sliced

2 cups chopped onions

4 tbsps unsalted dairy-free butter

Instructions:

1. Place pot insert and press sauté button.
2. Once pot is hot, add butter and lit melt.
3. Sauté mushrooms and onions for 5 minutes.
4. Season with lemon juice, pepper, salt, coconut aminos, paprika, and dill weed. Continue sautéing for 5 minutes more.
5. Stir in chicken broth and bring to a simmer for 5 minutes.
6. Meanwhile, in a bowl whisk well cassava flour and milk. Pour into pot and continue mixing until thickened.

7. Stir in sour cream and chopped parsley. Cook for 3 minutes or until heated through.
8. Serve and enjoy.

Nutrition information:

Calories per serving: 159; Carbohydrates: 15.7g; Protein: 5.2g; Fat: 9.4g; Sugar: 6.2g; Sodium: 698mg; Fiber: 3.1g

Delicious Salmon Chowder

Serves: 4
Cooking Time: 15 minutes

Ingredients:
1/4-lb goat cheese, shredded
1 cup cream of mushroom soup
1 cup A2 milk
1 16-oz cans salmon, drained
1 tsp dried dill weed
1 tsp ground black pepper
1 tsp salt
2 cups chicken broth
1 large sweet potato, peeled and cubed
1 tsp garlic powder
½ cup chopped celery
1 large onion, chopped
2 tbsps butter

Instructions:
1. Place pot insert and press sauté button.
2. Once pot is hot, add butter and let it melt.
3. Stir in sweet potato, celery, and onion. Sauté for 3 minutes.
4. Stir in mushroom soup, salmon, dill weed, pepper, salt, broth, and garlic powder. Mix well.
5. Press cancel, press manual button, cover Instant Pot, and seal. Set cooking time to 3 minutes.
6. Once done cooking allow for natural release for 5 minutes, do a quick release, and uncover pot.

7. Stir in cheese and stir to incorporate. Add milk and mix well. Cook until heated through.
8. Serve and enjoy.

Nutrition information:

Calories per serving: 396; Carbohydrates: 17.0g; Protein: 34.0g; Fat: 21.0g; Sugar: 7.0g; Sodium: 1886mg; Fiber: 2.1g

Vietnamese Style Chicken Soup (Pho)

Serves: 8
Cooking Time: 20 minutes

Ingredients:

Salt and pepper to taste

1 head bok choy chopped roughly

1 cup fresh cilantro

¼ cup fish sauce

1 lemon grass stalk, folded in 3-inch length and tied

4 cloves

1 cinnamon stick

1 black cardamom pod

1 tsp green coriander seed

1-inch ginger, peeled and roughly chopped

2 medium onions, quartered

4-lbs assorted chicken pieces, bone in and skin on

Fresh basil

6 cups water

Instructions:

1. Place pot insert.
2. Add all ingredients in pot except for fresh basil.
3. Press poultry button, cover Instant Pot, and seal. Set cooking time to 15 minutes.
4. Once done cooking allow for a complete natural release.
5. Remove chicken pieces, discard skin, shred, and discard bones. Equally place in 8 bowls. Evenly top chicken with fresh basil and set aside.
6. Strain broth and discard all herbs and spices. If desired, skim fat off.

7. Taste and adjust seasoning if needed. Ladle soup on top of chicken and basil bowls while boiling hot.
8. Serve and enjoy.

Nutrition information:

Calories per serving: 318; Carbohydrates: 5.4g; Protein: 52.6g; Fat: 8.5g; Sugar: 1.8g; Sodium: 898mg; Fiber: 1.3g

Manila Clam Soup

Serves: 4

Cooking Time: 20 minutes

Ingredients:

2-lbs Manila clams, brushed, cleaned and drained

1 stalk lemongrass, folded into 3-inch length and tied

6 gloves garlic, smashed, peeled, and chopped

2-inch long ginger, peeled and sliced thinly

1 large onion, sliced

¼ tsp salt

½ tsp cracked pepper

2 tsps fish sauce

4 cups water

1 tbsp olive oil

Instructions:

1. Place pot insert and press sauté button.
2. Once pot is hot, add oil.
3. Sauté garlic until fragrant, around 3 minutes.
4. Add clams and sauté for 5 minutes.
5. Add the rest of the ingredients and give it a good stir.
6. Press manual button, cover Instant Pot, and seal. Set cooking time to 3 minutes.
7. Once done cooking allow for natural release for 5 minutes, do a quick release, and uncover pot.
8. Serve and enjoy.

Nutrition information:

Calories per serving: 261; Carbohydrates: 15.6g; Protein: 35.4g; Fat: 5.7g; Sugar: 2.3g; Sodium: 2,230mg; Fiber: 0.8g

Fish Soup Recipe Philippines Style

Serves: 4

Cooking Time: 30 minutes

Ingredients:

2-lbs rockfish, sliced into 4

6 garlic cloves, smashed, peeled, and chopped

1 onion, chopped

1 stalk lemongrass, folded into 4 and tied

½ cabbage, quartered

2 stalks green onions, sliced white and greens divided

2-inch long ginger, peeled and sliced thinly

4 cups water

¼ tsp salt

½ tsp cracked pepper

1 tbsp fish sauce

1 tbsp olive oil

Instructions:

1. Place pot insert and press sauté button.
2. Once pot is hot, add oil and let it heat for 3 minutes.
3. Add garlic and sauté for a minute. Stir in onion, lemon grass, and ginger. Sauté for 5 minutes or until onions are soft and wilted.
4. Add 2 cups of water and deglaze pot. Bring to a simmer for 5 minutes.
5. Stir in salt, pepper, and fish sauce. Mix well. Add remaining water and mix.
6. Add fish and the white parts of the green onion.
7. Press cancel, press manual button, cover Instant Pot, and seal. Set cooking time to 2 minutes.

8. Once done cooking allow for natural release for 5 minutes, do a quick release, and uncover pot.
9. Add the cabbage while segregating each leaf as you add into pot. Add green onions and give it a good stir.
10. Cover and let it sit for 5 minutes until cabbage is tender.
11. Serve and enjoy.

Nutrition information:

Calories per serving: 294; Carbohydrates: 13.4g; Protein: 44.9g; Fat: 6.7g; Sugar: 5.5g; Sodium: 703mg; Fiber: 3.6g

Bacon-Hazelnut Cauliflower Soup

Serves: 6
Cooking Time: 20 minutes

Ingredients:

2 bay leaves

¾ cup heavy cream

6 cups low-sodium chicken broth

1/3 cup water

1 garlic clove, chopped finely

1 small onion, chopped

1 small fennel bulb, chopped

4 slices bacon

Salt and pepper to taste

2 tbsps olive oil or more

1 medium head cauliflower, cut into florets

½ cup hazelnuts

Instructions:

1. Blanch the hazelnuts by boiling 2 cups of water. Place boiling water in a bowl and add hazelnuts. Let it steep for two minutes and drain. Set aside.
2. Place pot insert and press sauté button.
3. Once pot is hot, add bacon strips and pan fry until crisped, around 8 minutes. Transfer to a plate and crumble, set aside.
4. Using bacon fat, stir fry garlic, onion, and fennel. Sauté for 3 minutes.
5. Add bay leaves, cauliflower, chicken broth, water, and hazelnuts.
6. Season with pepper and salt.
7. Press cancel, press manual button, cover Instant Pot, and seal. Set cooking time to 3 minutes.

8. Once done cooking allow for natural release for 5 minutes, do a quick release, and uncover pot.
9. Fish out bay leaves and discard.
10. With a handheld blender, puree soup until smooth. Stir in heavy cream and adjust seasoning if need.
11. Serve with a drizzle of olive oil and enjoy.

Nutrition information:

Calories per serving: 281; Carbohydrates: 12.4g; Protein: 10.6g; Fat: 22.9g; Sugar: 4.6g; Sodium: 234mg; Fiber: 3.5g

Lectin-Free Snack and Desserts Recipe

Gingerbread Cake in a Jar

Serves: 2
Cooking Time: 15 minutes

Ingredients:
2 eggs, lightly beaten
1 tbsp water
1 tsp apple cider vinegar
4 tsps honey
1 tsp baking powder
A pinch of allspice, cloves, and nutmeg spices
½ tsp cinnamon
1 tsp ground ginger
2 tbsps cassava flour
2 tbsps coconut flour
2 tbsps butter, softened

Instructions:
1. In a bowl, whisk well eggs and butter.
2. Add water, vinegar and honey. Mix again.
3. Stir in baking powder and spices. Mix well.
4. Add cinnamon, ginger, cassava flour, and coconut flour. Mix thoroughly.
5. Evenly divide into two mason jars. Cover mouth of Mason jar with foil securely.
6. Place pot insert, add a cup of water and place trivet.
7. Place jars on top of trivet.

8. Press cancel manual button, cover Instant Pot, and seal. Set cooking time to 5 minutes.

9. Once done cooking allow for a complete natural release.

10. Serve and enjoy.

Nutrition information:

Calories per serving: 316; Carbohydrates: 27.8g; Protein: 8g; Fat: 20.0g; Sugar: 13.4g; Sodium: 412mg; Fiber: 1.1g

Slow Cooker Applesauce

Serves: 8
Cooking Time: 6 Hours

Ingredients:
1 tsp cinnamon
¾ cup packed brown sugar
½ cup water
8 apples, peeled, cored, and sliced thinly

Instructions:
1. Place pot insert and add all ingredients in pot and mix well.
2. Press slow cook button, cover Instant Pot, and do not seal. Set cooking time to 6 hours on low.
3. Once done cooking allow to cool completely.
4. Serve and enjoy.

Nutrition information:
Calories per serving: 174; Carbohydrates: 45.6g; Protein: 0.5g; Fat: 0.3g; Sugar: 38.9g; Sodium: 8mg; Fiber: 4.5g

Serves: 6

Cooking Time: 15 minutes

Ingredients:

½ cup dark chocolate chips

1 tsp vanilla extract

½ cup melted coconut oil

1 cup applesauce

3 eggs

½ tsp baking powder

½ tsp baking soda

½ cup unsweetened cocoa powder

½ cup coconut sugar

½ cup tapioca flour

½ cup coconut flour

Instructions:

1. In a mixing bowl, whisk eggs. Stir in vanilla extract, coconut oil, and applesauce. Mix thoroughly.
2. Stir in baking powder, soda, and coconut sugar until thoroughly combined.
3. Add cocoa powder, tapioca flour, and coconut flour. Mix well.
4. Fold in chocolate chips.
5. Evenly divide into 1-pt Mason jars. Securely cover top with foil.
6. Place pot insert, add a cup of water, and place trivet.
7. Place Mason jars on top of trivet.
8. Press manual button, cover Instant Pot, and seal. Set cooking time to 10 minutes.
9. Once done cooking allow for natural release for 5 minutes, do a quick release, and uncover pot.
10. Let it cool completely.
11. Serve and enjoy.

Nutrition information:

Calories per serving: 366; Carbohydrates: 32.0g; Protein: 6.4g; Fat: 26.0g; Sugar: 14.6g; Sodium: 181mg; Fiber: 3.4g

Serves: 4

Cooking Time: 35 minutes

Ingredients:

3 extra large eggs

A pinch of salt

2 tsps vanilla extract

¼ cup sugar

1 cup heavy cream

1 cup A2 milk

2 tbsps water

½ cup white sugar

Instructions:

1. On medium high fire, add water and ½ cup white sugar in a nonstick pan and caramelize until golden brown, around 15 minutes. Continue swirling around.
2. Once caramel is done, transfer to a round and deep baking pan that fits inside your Instant Pot. Let the caramel cool.
3. In a large mixing bowl, whisk well eggs. Add a pinch of salt and whisk again.
4. Whisk in vanilla extract, ¼ cup sugar, heavy cream, and milk until thoroughly combined. Pour over caramel. Securely cover top of pan with foil.
5. Place pot insert, add a cup of water, and place trivet on bottom.
6. Place the baking pan on top of trivet.
7. Press manual button, cover Instant Pot, and seal. Set cooking time to 9 minutes.
8. Once done cooking allow for a complete natural release.
9. Uncover pot, let it cool completely.
10. Remove pan and refrigerate for at least 4 hours.

11. When ready to serve, remove foil, and gently use a knife to unstick flan from sides of pan.
12. Using a plate large, cover pan, and in one smooth motion turnover pan so that flan is now on the plate. Gently remove pan.
13. Serve and enjoy.

Nutrition information:

Calories per serving: 369; Carbohydrates: 35.9g; Protein: 10.6g; Fat: 20.1g; Sugar: 35.2g; Sodium: 166.5mg; Fiber: 0g

Instant Pot Deviled Eggs

Serves: 12

Cooking Time: 5 minutes

Ingredients:

¼ tsp salt

2 tsps lime juice

1 tbsp Dijon mustard

2 tbsps cilantro, minced

2 tbsps dairy-free butter, melted

¼ cup sour cream

1 cup water

12 organic eggs

Instructions:

1. Place pot insert, add water, and place trivet.
2. Place eggs on trivet.
3. Press manual button, cover Instant Pot, and seal. Set cooking time to 5 minutes.
4. Meanwhile, in a mixing bowl whisk well salt, lime juice, mustard, cilantro, butter, and sour cream until thoroughly blended.
5. Once done cooking do a quick release, uncover pot, and place eggs in an ice bath. Once cool enough to handle, peel eggs and slice in half. Remove yolk and place in mixing bowl and place boiled egg whites on a deviled egg tray.
6. Mix the yolk and sour cream mixture thoroughly and then evenly divide mixture on top of boiled egg whites.
7. Serve and enjoy.

Nutrition information:

Calories per serving: 82; Carbohydrates: 0.8g; Protein: 5.8g; Fat: 6.0g; Sugar: 0.2g; Sodium: 131mg; Fiber: 0.1g

Grandma's Tapioca Pudding

Serves: 4
Cooking Time: 20 minutes

Ingredients:

¼ tsp ground nutmeg

A pinch of sea salt

1 tsp vanilla extract

¼ cup maple syrup

1/3 cup tapioca pearls

1 13.5-oz can coconut milk

½ cup water

Instructions:

1. Place pot insert and mix all ingredients in pot.
2. Press manual button, cover Instant Pot, and seal. Set cooking time to 20 minutes.
3. Once done cooking do a quick release, and open pot.
4. Transfer pudding into a bowl and refrigerate until cool.
5. Serve and enjoy.

Nutrition information:

Calories per serving: 302; Carbohydrates: 27.4g; Protein: 2.1g; Fat: 22.0g; Sugar: 12.5g; Sodium: 55mg; Fiber: 0.1g

Mashed Sweet Potato Snack

Serves: 4
Cooking Time: 15 minutes

Ingredients:
2 medium sweet potatoes, washed
4 tbsps dairy-free butter
2 tbsps heavy cream
2 tbsps honey
A dash of salt

Instructions:
1. Place pot insert, add a cup of water, and place trivet on bottom.
2. Place washed sweet potatoes on trivet.
3. Press manual button, cover Instant Pot, and seal. Set cooking time to 5 minutes.
4. Once done cooking allow for a complete natural release.
5. Remove sweet potatoes from pot, peel, and transfer to a plate.
6. Mash sweet potato.
7. And for each sweet potato add 2 tbsps butter, 1 tbsp cream, 1 tbsp honey, and a dash of salt.
8. Mix well and enjoy.

Nutrition information:
Calories per serving: 186; Carbohydrates: 22.2g; Protein: 1.7g; Fat: 10.6g; Sugar: 13.2g; Sodium: 125mg; Fiber: 1.9g

Coconut Pandan Salad

Serves: 12

Cooking Time: 10 minutes

Ingredients:

1 cup coconut cream

½ cup + 2 tbsps sugar, divided

1 cup water

2 packages Knox unflavored gelatin

2 cups heavy whipping cream

½ tbsp pandan flavoring

1 jar nata de coco, preferably green color

Instructions:

1. Place pot insert and press sauté button.
2. Add a cup of water and 1 tbsp sugar and bring to a simmer. Once simmering, add 1 pouch of Knox gelatin and stir well to dissolve. Once dissolved, pour into a dish and add pandan flavoring. Mix well and let it cool in the fridge.
3. In same pot, add coconut cream, 1 tbsp sugar. Once simmering, add a pouch of Knox gelatin and dissolve. Once dissolved, pour into a separate container and let it cool in the fridge.
4. Meanwhile, in a large serving bowl, whisk whipping cream until stiff. Slowly adding ½ cup of sugar while beating continuously. Put in the fridge.
5. Once gelatin has set, slice thinly and add to bowl of cream.
6. Wash nata de coco and drain thoroughly. Add to bowl of cream. Fold to mix.
7. Serve and enjoy.

Nutrition information:

Calories per serving: 262.7; Carbohydrates: 30.1g; Protein: 3.0g; Fat: 15.3g; Sugar: 28.1g; Sodium: 89.4mg; Fiber: 0.5g

Pressure Cooked Chocolate Cheesecake

Serves: 8
Cooking Time: 35 minutes

Ingredients:
1 tsp vanilla extract
6-oz baking chocolate melted
¾ cup heavy cream
¼ cup sour cream
2 large egg yolks
1 large egg
1/3 cup unsweetened cocoa powder
¾ cup sugar
16-oz cream cheese
2 tbsps butter melted
1 ½ tbsps sugar
2 ½ tbsps unsweetened cocoa powder
¼ cup coconut flour
¼ cup almond flour

Instructions:
1. In a bowl mix well melted butter, 1 ½ tbsps sugar, 2 ½ tbsps cocoa powder, coconut flour, and almond flour. This will be the crust.
2. Line a 7-inch spring form pan with parchment paper and then press crumbs on bottom of pan.
3. In blender, blend all remaining ingredients until smooth and creamy. Pour over crust.
4. Securely cover bottom and top of pan with foil.
5. Place pot insert, add a cup of water, and place trivet on bottom.

6. Place foil wrapped pan on top of trivet.
7. Press manual button, cover Instant Pot, and seal. Set cooking time to 20 minutes.
8. Once done cooking allow for natural release for 15 minutes, do a quick release, and uncover pot. Let it cool completely in pot.
9. Remove from pot and then allow tool to room temperature.
10. Then refrigerate for at least four hours before serving.

Nutrition information:

Calories per serving: 413; Carbohydrates: 13g; Protein: 8g; Fat: 38g; Sugar: 2g; Sodium: 56mg; Fiber: 8g

Almond-Coconut Cake

Serves: 8
Cooking Time: 55 minutes

Ingredients:

½ cup heavy whipping cream

¼ cup butter melted

2 eggs

1 tsp apple pie spice

1 tsp baking powder

1/3 cup Truvia

½ cup unsweetened shredded coconut

1 cup almond flour

Instructions:

1. In a mixing bowl, whisk well eggs. Stir in cream butter, apple spice, baking powder, and Truvia until thoroughly mixed.
2. Stir in coconut and almond flour. Mix well.
3. Pour batter into prepared pan that fits inside Instant Pot. Cover top securely with foil.
4. Place pot insert, add a cup of water and place trivet on pot bottom.
5. Place pan on trivet.
6. Press manual button, cover Instant Pot, and seal. Set cooking time to 40 minutes.
7. Once done cooking allow for natural release for 15 minutes, do a quick release, and uncover pot.
8. Serve and enjoy.

Nutrition information:

Calories per serving: 236; Carbohydrates: 5g; Protein: 5g; Fat: 23g; Sugar: 0.7g; Sodium: 74mg; Fiber: 2g

CPSIA information can be obtained
at www.ICGtesting.com
Printed in the USA
LVOW09s0846040618

579487LV00003B/115/P